Divine Intervention is an amazing collection of miracle testimonies that will encourage the believer and challenge the skeptic as to the reality of God. The stories are as diverse as the people telling them. Daniel Fazzina is an excellent writer and does a wonderful job of bringing them all together. I know you will be moved by this book.

—JACK CANFIELD
Coauthor and originator, Chicken Soup for the Soul series

Divine Intervention is a fascinating, inspiring book that brings together modern-day miracle stories from all over the world. It is obvious from reading it that the God of the Bible is alive and still very active in human affairs today. Evidently Daniel Fazzina has been uniquely gifted and chosen to communicate this truth to our world today. I highly recommend *Divine Intervention* as a way to help strengthen your faith.

—PAT ROBERTSON
Founder, Christian Broadcasting Network

Divine Intervention, edited by Daniel Fazzina, is a must-read inspirational book containing powerful stories of God's grace, healing, and love in the midst of severe circumstances. This book will encourage you, inspire you, and set your heart on fire for Jesus Christ and His divine intervention. It is a joy to read. I highly recommend it.

—TED BAEHR
President, Christian Film & Television Commission
Publisher, www.movieguide.org

Your faith will be *challenged* and stimulated as you read these amazing true stories.

—SID ROTH
Host, *It's Supernatural!*

Divine Intervention by Daniel Fazzina focuses on sharing the testimonies of those whose encounter with Christ is meaningful, sometimes profound, and even miraculous. Daniel is an excellent interviewer whose follow-up questions bring even more insight to the matter at hand. His guest list is outstanding, which is another reflection of the quality of his work. And on top of it all, listening to Daniel's program or reading his

D1118069

books is a source of personal encouragement, as his topics invariably cause us to reflect on the great promise of Christ in us, "the hope of glory" (Col. 1:27). With Daniel we get a ministry and a ministry leader worthy of support!

—Dr. Frank Wright
President/CEO, Salem Communications
Former president/CEO, National Religious Broadcasters

It's obvious from Daniel Fazzina's *Divine Intervention* accounts that God speaks every day to a modern world. We need only listen.

—Lauren Green
Chief religion correspondent, Fox News

Divine Intervention is like Chicken Soup for the Soul meets the Bible. The amazing stories Daniel Fazzina features therein provide firsthand, modern-day evidence that God is still living and active in our lives today. Daniel skillfully gives us a front-row seat as to what He is doing with this incredible collection of personal miracle testimonies. Read this book and prepare to be awed and inspired!

—Deborah Smith Pegues
International speaker and best-selling author,
Emergency Prayers, 30 Days to Taming Your Tongue,
and *30 Days to Taming Your Finances*

Daniel Fazzina is a good-hearted dude! He inspires me. I think it is so cool that *Divine Intervention* contains small stories; huge, unbelievable stories; and everything in between. It is amazing to read how many miracles Jesus has done in people's lives. I love this book!

—Reggie "Fieldy" Arvizu
Bassist and founding band member, Korn

Daniel Fazzina is smart. He's prepared. He is direct and honest. His faith is the foundation that keeps him strong and trustworthy. Great guy to work with! The great thing about *Divine Intervention* is that it's about miracles. Do you believe in miracles? (*You know you want to...*)

—KEVIN SORBO
Actor, *God's Not Dead* and
Hercules: The Legendary Journeys

Daniel has a wonderful optimism that is founded on his experience and relationship with God. He is inspired, and he inspires me.

—SAM SORBO
Actress, author, radio personality

Daniel Fazzina has the rare talent of finding that perfect, once-in-a-lifetime, jaw-dropping miraculous story that leaves you crying, laughing, and praising God out loud. And just when you think nothing could top that, he goes on to do it again...and again...and again. I've been blessed and refreshed every time I've read a chapter of his book or heard an hour of his radio program. I wholeheartedly recommend his show and book as a tonic to grow your faith and confidence in the Lord.

—DR. KATHERINE ALBRECHT
Syndicated radio host, best-selling author, *Spychips*

As you enter into these pages, you will meet God face-to-face.

—KEN MANSFIELD
Author, speaker, former US manager of
The Beatles's Apple Records

Daniel Fazzina is a warm, funny guy with a real passion for people and God. He always sees the best in people and finds comfort in helping others achieve their goals. I love to listen to his radio show, as he finds the most amazing people with unbelievable stories (that are true). I always feel blessed after listening to Daniel. His *Divine Intervention* book brings such encouragement to readers. What a great way to recognize God in the midst of our problems!

—KIM ALEXIS
Supermodel, spokesperson, TV host

Daniel's stories are amazing and unbelievable!

—Frank Pastore
Former MLB pitcher, host of *The Frank Pastore Show*

Daniel Fazzina is making quite an impact for God with his *Divine Intervention* radio show and book. It's so inspiring to hear stories of how God has touched lives in so many unique ways. I highly recommend *Divine Intervention* to all those who want to be reminded of just how real and just how personal our God is.

—Robia LaMorte
Actress, *Buffy the Vampire Slayer*, and healing minister

These testimonies have truly inspired me...

—Ken Shamrock
World champion professional wrestler
and mixed martial artist

Daniel Fazzina is a man of true heart to inspire his audience worldwide by sharing the miracles of those he encounters. He is a complete gem to know.

—Jenn Gotzon
Actress, *Frost/Nixon* and *Doonby*

Divine Intervention is an amazing book that chronicles powerful personal testimonies of how Jesus has impacted the lives of ordinary people. From miraculous healings, to deliverances, answered prayers, and near-death experiences, this book has it all. If you are a believer in God and the supernatural, this book will encourage you in your faith. If you are a skeptic, you will be challenged. Either way, I know you will benefit from reading this incredible collection of powerful stories. God is still at work in the world today, and this book shows clear evidence of that! I highly recommend it!

—Dr. Gina Loudon
Author, host, *Smart Life With Dr. Gina*

Divine Intervention

Divine Intervention

daniel fazzina

CHARISMA
HOUSE

Most CHARISMA HOUSE BOOK GROUP products are available at special quantity discounts for bulk purchase for sales promotions, premiums, fund-raising, and educational needs. For details, write Charisma House Book Group, 600 Rinehart Road, Lake Mary, Florida 32746, or telephone (407) 333-0600.

DIVINE INTERVENTION by Daniel Fazzina
Published by Charisma House
Charisma Media/Charisma House Book Group
600 Rinehart Road
Lake Mary, Florida 32746
www.charismahouse.com

This book or parts thereof may not be reproduced in any form, stored in a retrieval system, or transmitted in any form by any means—electronic, mechanical, photocopy, recording, or otherwise—without prior written permission of the publisher, except as provided by United States of America copyright law.

Unless otherwise noted, all Scripture quotations are from the New King James Version of the Bible. Copyright © 1979, 1980, 1982 by Thomas Nelson, Inc., publishers. Used by permission.

Scripture quotations marked GNT are from the Good News Translation® in Today's English Version-Second Edition) Copyright © 1992 American Bible Society by American Bible Society. Used by permission.

Scripture quotations marked NAS are from the New American Standard Bible, copyright © 1960, 1962, 1963, 1968, 1971, 1972, 1973, 1975, 1977, 1995 by The Lockman Foundation. Used by permission. (www.Lockman.org)

Scripture quotations marked NCV are from The Holy Bible, New Century Version. Copyright © 1987, 1988, 1991 by Word Publishing, Dallas, Texas 75039. Used by permission.

Scripture quotations marked NIV are taken from the Holy Bible, New International Version®, NIV®. Copyright © 1973, 1978, 1984, 2011 by Biblica, Inc.™ Used by permission of Zondervan. All rights reserved worldwide. www.zondervan.com The "NIV" and "New International Version" are trademarks registered in the United States Patent and Trademark Office by Biblica, Inc.™

Copyright © 2014 by Daniel Fazzina
All rights reserved

Cover design by Bill Johnson
Design Director: Justin Evans

Visit the author's website at www.divineinterventionradio.com.

Library of Congress Cataloging-in-Publication Data:
Divine intervention / [edited by] Daniel Fazzina. -- First edition.
    pages cm
  ISBN 978-1-62136-554-9 (trade paper) -- ISBN (invalid) 978-1-62136-
555-6 (e-book)
  1. Christian converts--Biography. 2. Conversion--Christianity--Biography.
3. Christian biography. I. Fazzina, Daniel.
  BV4930.D58 2014
  270.8'20922--dc23
  [B]
                                  2014018612

Some names have been changed to protect the individuals' privacy.

First edition

14 15 16 17 18 — 9 8 7 6 5 4 3 2 1
Printed in the United States of America

This book is dedicated to Jesus Christ, with love and appreciation. Thank You for Your precious gifts of extravagant love, abundant life, and amazing grace. I pray You will help me to serve You faithfully all the days of my life.

Contents

Write down for the coming generation
what the LORD has done, so that people
not yet born will praise him.

PSALM 102:18, GNT

Acknowledgments

*T*HIS BOOK WAS a labor of love for me. When God put it on my heart in 2005 to share the stories of God's miraculous intervention in people's lives, I did not envision then that this undertaking would become a book and a radio show, or that it would impact so many lives. I am so humbled and grateful that God has given me so many stories of His awesome miracles that they couldn't be contained in one book. I am so happy that this project was birthed. Working on it has been inspirational, cathartic, and a tremendous honor.

I want to thank everyone who aided me in any way, whether materially with content for the book, spiritually with prayers for it, or emotionally with words of encouragement. This book would not have been possible without the help and contributions of so many people.

First and foremost, I would like to thank God, the Lord Jesus Christ, who is the very reason for my writing this book and for whom I exist. Thank You for Your love, mercy, and grace. You truly are the King of kings and Lord of lords. No one can compare to You. You have blessed me beyond measure, and it is my joy to honor You in all I do.

To my magnificent bride, Sahani, the love of my life—thank you for your unwavering love and support, your prayers for me and this project, and for always challenging me to be a better man. Your worth is far above rubies.

To my parents, Joe and Gwen—thank you for your love, generosity, and care for me; and for pointing me to Jesus at a young age.

To my grandma Arline—thank you for demonstrating a lifestyle of selfless giving. You are truly an inspiration to me. I am blessed to have you as a grandmother.

To my wonderful family—I thank God for each and every one of you. I am blessed to have you in my life.

To Amma, Thatha, Mama, Shain, and my entire extended family—I truly appreciate your love and generosity in welcoming me into your family as your own. *Bohome istuti!*

To Lorraine Zito and Patricia Duffield, my second mom and second aunt—thank you so much for your generosity and support, for believing in me, and for helping me get *Divine Intervention* off the ground. This book would not have been possible without your help. May God richly bless you both for your kindness toward me.

To Allen and Leah Cuffey—thank you for your friendship and your amazing generosity in helping me to launch *Divine Intervention Radio*. I look forward to many more years of partnership, fellowship, and friendship. God bless you both.

To Valerie Lowe—thank you for believing in me and this project, and for helping me connect with the right people to bring it to fruition. You are a blessing!

To Adrienne Gaines and all the wonderful people at Charisma House—thank you for all your hard work in making this book a reality.

To Bruce Barbour—thank you for your generosity and sage advice in working with me to help this novice author navigate the world of publishing and contracts.

To all the amazing people who contributed their testimonies for this book—may the Lord Jesus Christ bless you for publicly acknowledging and honoring Him, as He says in His Word:

> Therefore whoever confesses Me before men, him I will also confess before My Father who is in heaven. But whoever denies Me before men, him I will also deny before My Father who is in heaven.
> —MATTHEW 10:32–33

Liz Alberti; Elisheva the wandering *goy*—your passion for Yeshua and Israel are gifts to those around you. Thanks for sharing your amazing life story with me.

Zachariah Anani—you are bold and fearless. Your testimony is amazing, and your passion to follow Jesus despite persecution and danger is inspiring. I am honored to call you friend.

George Baah, my African brother—your zeal for Jesus and desire for everyone to know Him are contagious. Thank you for being a light to the world.

Maria Baron—your humility and passion for Jesus are an inspiration. Thank you so much for sharing with the world the miracles that Jesus has done in your life.

Libby Baron—the love of God overflows from your huge heart. Thank you for your compassion and desire to help people come to know Jesus. You are an amazing person and a tremendous blessing.

Joshua Bender, artist and evangelist—I appreciate so much how real you are. Thank you for your friendship and your sincere desire to live for God.

Jonathan Bernor—you are larger than life in so many ways. Your passion for prayer and evangelism are contagious. God bless you, my brother. I am proud to call you friend.

Anupam Bhomia—your faith, perseverance, and desire to know Jesus and to make Him known to those around you are refreshing. Thank you for sharing your story.

Orlando Crespo—I appreciate your sensitivity and genuine compassion. Christ's love is so evident in your life. Thank you for investing your life serving Jesus and college students.

Steven Delopoulos—your friendship and music have brought much joy into my life. Thank you for using your gifts for God's glory and for contributing to this book.

Robby Dilmore—the joy of the Lord is evident in your life. Your fun and jovial demeanor, along with your passion for Jesus, is so refreshing. Thank you for allowing me to share your miracle testimony in this book.

Carol Dixon—your father's life and sacrifice for both God and country will forever be remembered. Jacob DeShazer has earned his eternal reward, and I look forward to meeting him in heaven someday. Thank you for allowing me to share his story.

Mark Excel—I am so happy to have met you and become your friend. Your genuineness, humility, and passion for Jesus are so refreshing. Thank you for sharing your amazing story with me.

Gwen Fazzina, Mom—I so appreciate your love and generosity. Thank you for being there for me and helping to instill in me an appreciation for learning. I love you.

Joseph Fazzina, father and friend—thank you so much for leading by example, demonstrating for me the right way to live, and pointing me to God throughout my life. You are a good man and great father to me. I love you.

Kevin Frohlich—your life is an amazing testimony of the transforming power of Jesus Christ. Thank you for sharing the love God gave you with the world. You are an amazing man of God.

Derrick Holmes—your maturity, faith, and hope throughout your trials and suffering inspire me. It is an honor to know you.

J. Jackson—I so appreciate your humor, incredible musical talent, and your burden to reach the lost for Christ. Your unique ministry is very much needed and a blessing to so many people. Keep up the great work for the Lord. You are a dear brother to me.

Mathew John—your life is a testimony to the Lord's faithfulness. Thank you for your desire to make that known to the world and for walking by faith, not by sight.

Dani Johnson—you are a light on a hill and one of the most amazing people I have ever met. I so appreciate your openness and honesty, your passion for Jesus and to see people prosper, and your willingness to be used by God. You are touching so many lives, and I am honored to know you. Thank you so much for sharing your life and testimony with me.

Richard Jones, pastor, teacher, and friend—thank you for your friendship, guidance, servant's heart, and true humility. You are a blessing.

Rick Jordan, faithful servant to the body of Christ—the love and gratitude you exude are so evident, and your TV shows are a blessing to so many. Thank you for all your work for the kingdom and for sharing the many amazing miracles God has done in your life.

Penny Kassay—your commitment to live a godly, Spirit-filled life of prayer and evangelism are inspiring to me. Thank you for contributing to this work.

Fred Klemm—it is such a joy to see your excitement for what Jesus has done in your life. Thank you so much for sharing your story with me.

John Kruse, cousin and brother—your sense of humor is refreshing, and God's providence is evident in your life. Thank you for your generosity in sharing your story.

Billy Lamont, gifted wordsmith and true friend—your passion for life, spirit of humility, and generosity inspire me. Thank you for your friendship and encouragement.

Marilyn Laszlo, gutsy and gracious—your obedience in following Jesus to the jungles of New Guinea is truly inspiring. Thanks for sharing your story and your life.

Denise Lotierzo-Block, a precious soul—I so appreciate how real you are and your grateful and generous spirit. Thank you for sharing your testimony in this book. God bless you.

Jeff Markin, my fellow Long Islander—I am blown away by the miracle God has done in your life. It is a joy to see you embrace your experience and grow in God's grace through it. You have inspired, and will continue to encourage, many people. Thank you for your willingness to share your story with me and the world. So happy to have you as a friend.

George McCormack—I thank you and Martha so much for your willingness to share the wonderful miracles God has done in your lives. It is a blessing to know you.

Ema McKinley—God's love and light radiate from you, and I am amazed at your faithfulness and joy despite your suffering. Thank you for embracing this new journey God has you on, and for allowing me to include your incredible testimony in this book. You are an inspiration and a blessing, and I am so happy to know you and call you friend.

Eric Metaxas, my fellow writer and Northeasterner—I love your humor and wit. Your excellence in writing and public speaking are truly gifts to the body of Christ. So happy to know you.

Jeffrey D. Miller—you are such a great storyteller and so much fun to interact with. Your passion for Yeshua and making Him known are inspiring. Thank you for contributing to this work, my friend.

Jean Nolting, dear friend—your life is an incredible testimony, filled with so many miracles. You are obviously a dearly beloved daughter of our King. God bless you for sharing your amazing life with the world.

Jules Ostrander, cowboy and prophet—the spiritual fire and excitement you have for Jesus are an inspiration. Thank you for blessing New York and America with your message.

Joe Paskewich—thank you for your friendship, encouragement, and support. You are unique and gifted in so many ways, and God has used you mightily in Connecticut and beyond. Your story is such an inspiration. Thank you for sharing it with me and with the world.

Regine Paul Jones, dear sister and friend—the love of Jesus is so manifest in you that you light up a room when you walk in. I have so enjoyed our friendship and working relationship over the past fifteen-plus years. I know it was no accident that we met. Thank you for sharing your testimony with me for this book. You are a blessing.

Joe Pinto—thank you for using your gifts and talents to faithfully serve God's people and for your friendship through the years. You are a blessing to so many, especially to me.

Sandra Rivera—the joy of the Lord is so manifest in your life. Thank you for your faithfulness to God and for your desire to share Jesus with those around you.

Mark Russak, intelligent and humble—thank you so much for your graciousness, for standing for the truth, and for allowing the world to know about the wonderful miracle the Lord did in your life. I'm proud to call you friend.

Kamal Saleem—it is an honor and a privilege to know you and to learn of the incredible change God has made in you. You are a true friend. I so appreciate your courage, humility, and passion for our Lord and King. You are precious in God's sight and a true ambassador of His kingdom. Thank you for following Jesus's call and for allowing me to use your story in this book. God bless you always.

Dayalan Sanders—I so appreciate your genuine, humble spirit. God will richly reward you for your commitment to Jesus and the orphaned children of Sri Lanka. Thank you for sharing your story for this book.

Govind Sathiya Seelan—you are a passionate man of God, and your testimony is amazing. It is obvious that God called you to be a minister and to reach your people with the message of Jesus Christ. It is an honor to know you. Thank you for sharing your incredible life with me and with the world.

Steven Sebyala—your humility and passion to win Africa for Jesus are inspiring. Great will be your treasure in heaven. Thank you for sharing part of your life with me.

Anton Stubbs—you are a gifted, courageous leader and have been both a friend and an inspiration to me since our days in college together. Thank you for letting Jesus shine through you and for serving your country and fellow man. I am honored to call you friend and brother.

Grant Stubbs—I am honored to have met you and thankful that you have allowed me to share your incredible miracle story with the world in this book. Your love for the Lord and desire to see Him glorified through your life are evident. Thank you for your graciousness and service to the King.

Joanna Swanson—you are a shining jewel made perfect through God's grace. The love of God shines through you, and your care and compassion for the broken and hurting are inspiring. I am blessed to know you.

Dennis Swift—you are an inspiration, both for the way God moves supernaturally in your life and for the awesome archaeological research you have done to support the Bible. Your passion for letting God's truth and history be known is so refreshing. Thank you for your service to Jesus and your fellow man. I am so happy we met.

Owen Wilson, "O. B. Angels"—it was evident that angels were with you during your microlight flight that fateful day with Grant. I appreciate your humility and desire to see God glorified through your testimony. Thanks so much for allowing me to share your story in this book. I am so glad we connected!

Julie Woodley, God's wildflower—I love your joy and enthusiasm and how you see every opportunity as an adventure from God. You embrace it all with childlike glee and wonder. God's love flows through you so powerfully, and I am humbled and honored to call you friend.

Introduction

As I go through my daily life, I meet all kinds of people from many different backgrounds. I have experienced the supernatural work of God in my life many times, and I often wonder if other people have had similar experiences. Being curious and inquisitive by nature, I frequently ask people I meet, "Have you ever witnessed or experienced a miracle or a divine intervention?"

Nearly everyone I ask has a story about something that happened in their life that defied natural explanation, something considered to be a miracle. It could be a near-death experience, a close call in which they should have been killed, a dramatic healing, or even an answered prayer that gave them the help they needed at just the right time. Some people's entire lives seem to be one long sequence of divine interventions and miracles.

Yet for others, these types of occurrences seem to be totally outside their experience. I often wonder why that is. Maybe they don't recognize a miracle when they see one. Maybe they just haven't experienced one yet, but their time will come. Whatever the reason, the fact is, for some people divine interventions are outside their world altogether. When I asked one friend if he had ever experienced a miracle, he responded that he never had—and even questioned the very existence of miracles.

"After all," he reasoned, "if the miracles and divine interventions like the ones written in the Bible are true, they would still be happening today. How come I've never seen one?"

A fair question, undoubtedly. It was this line of reasoning that became the very purpose for my writing *Divine Intervention*. In my experience miracles and divine interventions like those recorded in the Bible are still happening—today! People just need to know about them.

During the short time I have walked this planet, I've been blessed to meet some very interesting people who have experienced God's hand in some powerful ways. I do not believe that these meetings were coincidences or chance encounters; rather, I believe they were divine appointments.

I do not think it is a coincidence, for example, that I have met three people who have been shot in the head and lived to tell about it. Nor do I think it accidental that I happen to know three people who miraculously recovered from a coma and paralysis after doctors said they should be dead or, at best, vegetables. I do not chalk up to serendipity the fact that a good friend of mine from college, who was born a paraplegic, was able to miraculously get up out of his wheelchair and walk for the first time at age seven after being prayed for in the name of Jesus.

I have experienced God's intervention in my own life many times, including two dramatic healings—one from a painful, chronic back condition and one from a large cancerous tumor that threatened my life. I've met people who have experienced God's intervention in all types of ways—not just through healings.

In fact, these experiences seem to be quite common in the lives of many people who are sincere followers of Jesus Christ, no matter what denomination they are affiliated with. Their stories inspire hope and faith and need to be told. They are a testament to the fact that Jesus Christ is alive and well and still working among us every day. I believe God allowed me to meet these people for that reason—so I could share these true stories of His goodness and power.

I am continually blown away by the incredibly passionate, gifted, and generous people God has sent my way. They have been selfless, transparent, and vulnerable, and in many cases have bared their souls with the single goal of encouraging you, dear reader, to have faith in the Lord Jesus Christ—Immanuel, "God with us."

Every testimony in this book is a firsthand account of an actual event or events, told to me by the people who experienced them. In these pages you will find stories of divine healing, deliverance, guidance, protection, and provision, and of how people came to faith in the Lord Jesus Christ. Some of the stories qualify for more than one of these categories. Some are single incidents, some are a sequence of events, and some could even be considered mini-biographies. But each is a story of how God intervened in human affairs.

If you do not believe in God or have never experienced a miracle or a divine intervention, it is my prayer that this book will be your introduction to the many ways that God does intervene in people's lives daily. If you already believe, then may this book help strengthen your faith in the One who loves you and gave His life for you. Wherever you are in your journey, may this book be a blessing and an encouragement to you. Open wide your eyes, heart, and mind—and get ready to witness the miraculous!

—Daniel Fazzina
www.divineinterventionradio.com

1

God Is Enough

Whoever then humbles himself as this child,
he is the greatest in the kingdom of heaven.

MATTHEW 18:4, NAS

MY NAME IS Marilyn Laszlo. I was born in 1933 in Valparaiso, Indiana. I spent twenty-four years as a missionary in Papua New Guinea, living and working in the jungle among the Sepik Iwam people.

When I arrived in Hauna village in 1967, they had no written language. My job was to learn their language, work with them to develop a written alphabet, teach them to read and write, and eventually translate the Bible into their language. By God's grace, I was able to do all of this and more. God performed many miracles while I was on the mission field. I'll relate one amazing divine intervention here.

One of the first things I had to do was teach my translator helpers, who were just young boys, how to run our canoe's outboard motor. Every three months we went downriver one hundred ten miles to the airstrip at Ambunti for supplies. I'm an Indiana farm girl; this was way over my head to do alone. I didn't know the river and was always running into sand banks and having motor trouble. Those boys knew the river and how to avoid sandbanks, whirlpools, and submerged logs.

Like any boys anywhere in the world, they were interested in speed. A canoe that goes twenty miles per hour was exciting! Everyone wanted to run the motor. I was training eight boys all between the ages of eleven and eighteen—except for Joel, who was older. I taught them things such as how to change the spark plugs, clean the fuel line, repair the propeller, and what equipment to bring on trips: extra spark plugs, pins, propellers, spare fuel lines, tools, etc.

I told them, "OK, we're preparing to go downriver for supplies. It takes all day to get downriver, so we need four tanks of gas. Coming back, we'll need five tanks because we'll be going against the current."

The trip downriver was blissful. The boys took turns guiding the dugout and changing the gas tank when one ran dry. As I watched them, I silently prayed, "Lord, thank You for these special young men. Help me respect Your chosen translators as they deserve."

When we reached Ambunti, the supplies we ordered were stacked and ready for us.

We awoke before dawn the next morning for the exhausting job of carefully loading and balancing the canoe.

We left for Hauna around 10:00 a.m.

"We'll have a bright moon," Joel said.

"Plenty of gas?"

"Plenty."

On the way back night fell, but the moon rose full and bright, illuminating the river. As the boys piloted the canoe, the motor's whirring lulled me to sleep.

When we passed Fukai village, an hour from Hauna, the motor stopped. The sudden silence awakened me. We were drifting; the current was about five miles per hour, pushing us back.

There was much commotion in the back of the canoe. "What are you guys doing?" I asked.

"We're having motor trouble," they said.

"Did you check the fuel line? Is it dirty?" I asked.

"The fuel line is fine."

"Did you change the spark plugs?"

"The spark plugs are OK."

I thought, "Oh, my goodness."

We were in the middle of the jungle at night—if we couldn't get the motor started, I knew the only way out of there would be to drift back to the airstrip. There were no service stations along the river, and we couldn't paddle a sixty-foot canoe against the current. I knew that it would take us more than *four days* to drift back to the airstrip from that part of the river. I wasn't looking forward to that.

Joel finally spoke. "We're out of strong water." (*Strong water* is the Sepik term for gas.)

"It never takes more than five tanks to get home from Ambunti!" I exclaimed. "How many did we have?"

"Four," they replied.

"*Four?*" I blurted. "You only loaded four tanks of strong water for the trip home? You know we need *five* tanks to make it upriver! Why didn't you follow instructions?"

I was angry.

"What are we going to do?" I questioned. "Just *what* are we going to do?"

I'm going on and on. When you're angry, you speak the language more fluently—the words just bubble out. I don't want to tell you what I said to those guys.

Anyway, they were young, but they all had become Christians—they all had asked Jesus into their lives. Finally, they said, "Marilyn, just fasten your mouth and sit there."

"Fine," I said. "I'm just going to sit here. But what are we going to do?"

"We'll ask Papa God," they replied.

I sat there angrily brushing away the cloud of mosquitoes that had engulfed our canoe, and said, "You're going to pray? Oh, well, that's just great! Just what are we going to pray about? We're out of gas!"

They said, "Marilyn, we've been translating in Genesis and other places. It says in God's carving that Papa God sees everywhere. He knows all about us, so Papa God can see that we're in trouble here on the river."

Those eight boys gathered around the four empty gas tanks, laid their hands on the barrels and the motor, and began praying. "Oh, Papa, we're in trouble. Papa, we're in a lot of trouble with Marilyn." (They had that right.) "But Papa, You created the stars in heaven. You said, 'Be there,' and they started shining. You created the moon, clouds, and everything up there. Papa, none of it ever falls down. It takes great power to hold those stars up. If one ever fell, it would kill us and crush every tree."

A calm came over me as I watched them in the moonlight of the jungle. Tears began flowing down my cheeks.

They continued: "You have much power. Your Jesus walked on water.

3

What is it for You to make our motor push us home? It's nothing to You, Papa God!"

Joel pulled the starter rope. "Papa God, You're enough! We don't need any gas!" The engine sputtered.

"Please, Papa God! Give power to this motor!" he shouted. Joel pulled the rope again, and the motor started! The boys shouted with joy and beat the sides of the canoe like a huge drum.

"Thank You!" they shouted. "Papa God has power!"

Amazingly, those eight boys prayed, they pulled the rope on that motor, and it started. I thought it was running on a trickle of gas and fumes, and as I waited for it to stop, I remembered the time Jesus used a child to teach a lesson to His disciples who were worrying about who would become the greatest in the kingdom. Matthew 18:3–4 says, "Unless you are converted and become like children, you will not enter the kingdom of heaven. Whoever then humbles himself as this child, he is the greatest in the kingdom of heaven" (NAS). That motor kept running. We went for nearly an hour, all the way back to our village—*without one drop of fuel.*

Marilyn Laszlo is a sought-after speaker for conferences, retreats, colleges, banquets, and other events. After living twenty-four years in a jungle village, translating God's Word for people who had no written language, she returned home to her native Indiana. Today she continues to seek God's guidance and follow Him in new ways. With a twinkle in her eye and a mischievous smile, she enjoys recounting times when she heard God's call, argued with Him about who was in charge, ate grubs—and witnessed miracles. For more information, write marilynlaszlo@comcast.net or visit www.laszlomissionleague.com.

2

Jesus: A Friend to Terrorists

If My people who are called by My name
will humble themselves, and pray and
seek My face, and turn from their wicked
ways, then I will hear from heaven, and
will forgive their sin and heal their land.

2 CHRONICLES 7:14

Y NAME IS Kamal Saleem. I was born into a large Sunni Muslim family in Beirut, Lebanon, in 1957. My mother taught me Islamic radicalism, and my father taught me to hate Christians and Jews. As a child I was recruited by the Palestinian Liberation Organization (PLO) and completed my first mission at age seven, smuggling weapons into Israel through tunnels in the Golan Heights. During my many years of training, I mastered many forms of terrorist tactics. I was trained in assault camps to use weapons such as AK-47s, grenades, and Katyusha rockets. As a child I could shoot mortars and antiaircraft guns, and even slit throats.

I eventually became a powerful warlord, participating in many conflicts, from fighting Jews in Israel to Christians in Lebanon to Russians in Afghanistan. I was sold out for jihad and worked with and for notorious figures such as Yasser Arafat, Saddam Hussein, and Muammar Gaddafi. As a young man I left the Middle East to enter my mission field: America. I had a tremendous passion to convert as many Americans as possible to Islam. I implemented my plan and converted many people.

In 1985 my world was turned upside down by a divine intervention in the form of a serious car accident. God used this traumatic event, and what followed, to transform my life. I will share how God changed me from a radical Muslim terrorist to a Christian minister and lover of people.

I came to America on a student visa, not divulging my true intentions. I'd go from mosque to mosque in America teaching the jihadist mentality: how to become warriors for Allah. I was also fund-raising for the PLO.

One day, as I was driving down the highway in the left lane, a car came from the right lane and cut in front of me. I hit the brakes so hard that my car spun to the left and went into oncoming traffic. At that instant a tractor-trailer hit me full force, breaking my car in half. I was ejected and landed on my neck in a muddy ditch. I couldn't move. I felt my body; I wasn't paralyzed, but I was stunned from the impact.

I thought, "Allah, *rabbi wah-maw lay* (my lord and king), this isn't even my fault! Why did you allow this to happen?" I was Allah's chosen warrior advancing Islam, and I was in a mud hole. Suddenly a man came running, and he knelt down and looked at me.

"Don't worry," he said. "Everything will be OK. I called the ambulance, and it's on the way." He then took his white shirt off and cleaned the mud from my face. He was smiling. That smile was creepy to me.

The ambulance came and took me to the hospital. The first two doctors I met in the hospital said almost the same thing to me, word for word. "Everything will be OK. Don't worry about anything. We'll take care of you." They also had those same creepy smiles. It was very strange.

On my fifth day in the hospital the first guy who helped me on the street visited me. As he was checking on me, the first doctor who met me in the emergency room walked in. They looked at each other and started laughing and calling each other by name, saying, "How are you doing?" Then the second doctor entered, and they started hugging each other and telling each other, "I love you."

I'm thinking: "Oh, my God! They're not just Christians; they're *foofy* Christians! What's wrong with you people? You don't hug another man and tell him you love him!"

They came to my bedside saying, "Your bill is over $60,000. We must get you out of the hospital." One of the doctors took me to his house and gave me his best room. His wife was a nurse, and she took care of me. I had a broken collarbone, two cracked vertebrae, and multiple other injuries. The whole family loved me. Their children would climb on my bed, lay their little hands on me, and pray that Jesus would heal me.

I later learned those doctors belonged to a professional Christian businessmen's association. About fifty men would meet weekly, put me in a circle, hold hands, and pray that Jesus would heal me, love me, take care of me, and change my life. They also put a basket in front of me, dropped checks in it, and paid my medical bills. They didn't just love me, they set the example for me. They never said to me: "You're a Muslim. You're an infidel. You don't deserve this life. Go back home, you foreigner!" or anything like that. They loved me unconditionally and showed me how it's done.

I thought, "These people I hate—they're good people! They're loving, kind, and pure." Later I read in the Bible that Jesus said, "Love your enemies, do good to those who hate you" (Luke 6:27–28). Islam says, "Treat your enemy harshly and lie in wait for them with every trick" (Sura 9, At-Tawbah). One said hate, the other said the opposite: love.

Suddenly I became a *foofy* hugger and started telling these people I loved them. Something came over me. I couldn't fight it. How do you fight love? Jesus said, "A new commandment I give to you, that you love one another; as I have loved you, that you also love one another. By this all will know that you are My disciples" (John 13:34–35). He sealed it right there.

These people did what they did, and it was amazing. I was with them for several weeks recovering. I had a cast on my neck, hip, and shoulder. I was entrusted with their house keys and car keys. I babysat for them, and they took care of me. They paid my bills, bought me a car to replace the one I lost in the accident, and put me back on my feet.

One day the doctor said, "Now you're well enough to go home." When I returned to my apartment, I was so confused. Is Islam reality, or is Christianity reality? I didn't know what to do. I learned that Christians have a relationship with God. They speak to God and hear from God. They say, "God told me this. God healed me after I prayed. God provided finances. God did miracles in my life." In Islam we didn't have any of this. There are no miracles in Islam. Allah is up there, and you're down here. You do all you can, hoping Allah will accept you.

With this, I fell on my knees, facing east (as a good Muslim boy), raised my hands toward heaven, and said, "Allah, Allah, *rabbi wah-maw lay* (my lord and king), why did you allow this to happen to me? I've served you! I've changed the world for your glory! I love you and do everything for you! Why put me among the Christians? I'm confused! These people have this thing called 'love' that I don't know how to fight! Allah, speak to me! I need to know you're real! I need to know you care, that you give me healing, just like they prayed to their God, and they were healed!"

Allah didn't speak. In my distress I thought, "Maybe I was wrong?" I realized that everything I'd lived and worked for was false, valueless, and was exalting nobody. I thought, "I can't go back and tell my family what happened. They'd shoot me in the head in five seconds if I told them I was considering leaving Islam."

I thought dying as a warrior would be best. Then I thought, "Maybe I'll ask once more."

"Allah, speak to me!" I prayed. "Tell me you care and that you love me! I want to know you! I want to hear your voice!" I was seeking Allah desperately because after that was a point of no return. I didn't hear anything, so I went to reach for my gun to put a bullet in the right place.

As I arose, I heard a voice. It was strong, yet gentle, so loving, so kind. It said: "Kamal, the Muslims, Christians, and Jews believe and pray to the God of Father Abraham. Why don't you give the God of Father Abraham, Isaac, and Jacob a chance?" When I heard this, I knew it was real. I didn't need that invitation twice.

I fell on my knees facing east, raised my hands toward heaven, and said, "God of Father Abraham! If You're real, speak to me!" That was all I had to ask. My eyes, ears, and heart were open. Suddenly I saw Him! I saw the wind engulfing Him and praising Him! I heard the birds of the earth exalting and praising Him! He was wearing what resembled a Jewish shawl, and I saw holes in His hands.

"Who are You?" I asked.

He said, "I am that I am."

Totally confused, I said, "I'm a man of little understanding. Please, what is that supposed to mean?"

He said: "I am the Alpha; I am the Omega. I am the beginning; I am the end. I am everything in between. I have created you. Before I created the foundation of the earth, I knew you and called you by name. I formed you in your mother's womb. You are *My* warrior; you are not their warrior. Rise up!"

As I arose, my body was intact! I had a miracle healing through this God I never knew before! My neck, arm, and collarbone were healed! Suddenly I knew He was Christ, the Messiah, Son of the living God. I knew He was my Lord and King, the God who speaks, who lives, who reigns, and whose kingdom is everlasting.

I said, "I will live and die for You, my Lord!"

He said, "Do not die for me. I have already died for you, that you may live." In that moment I realized I didn't have to be a martyr anymore.

I said, "I will go and pull them by the skin of their teeth and make them Christians."

"The harvest is plentiful, but the workers are few," He said. "Be My ambassador."

I started jumping and shouting: "I'm God's ambassador! I'm God's ambassador!" I surrendered my life to Jesus Christ, and today I'm completely changed. I risk my life daily for His glory, honor, and kingdom.

This is my story. I lived my life to die for the cause of Allah, jihad, and Islam. But the true God revealed Himself to me and showed me that what I was doing was wrong. Today I live for Jesus Christ: the way, the truth, and the life.

If you're a Muslim and aren't sure if Allah is real, I'd advise you to say, "God of Father Abraham, Isaac, and Jacob, if You're real, speak to me. Guide me. Show me the truth." That's all you have to do. It's an invitation to the truth, and the truth will set you free. You don't have to convert from Islam. Just call on the God of Father Abraham, Isaac, and Jacob, and He'll show you things beyond your expectation.

 **Kamal Saleem** is an ordained Christian minister. His amazing testimony of God's transforming power, as well as his intimate knowledge of Islamist tactics and conquest plans, make him a popular speaker and media guest. He has shared his story in churches, synagogues, and Muslim communities, on major media programs and Ivy League campuses, and with US military leaders, security experts, and law-enforcement specialists. Kamal is married to an American Christian woman and lives in the United States. For more information, write kamal.saleem@koomeministries.com, or visit www.koomeministries.com or www.kamalsaleem.com.

3

Rise and Walk

Peter said, "...In the name of Jesus Christ of
Nazareth, rise up and walk." And he took him
[the paralytic] by the right hand and lifted
him up, and immediately his feet and ankle
bones received strength. So he, leaping up,
stood and walked and entered the temple with
them—walking, leaping, and praising God.

ACTS 3:6–8

MY NAME IS Dr. George Baah. I was born in 1975 in Ghana, Africa. My father was a civil servant and my mother a teacher. I was born with meningitis and, according to my mother, when I was born my hair was falling out and I was very sickly. I was in a big hospital with many others with meningitis, and there was no medication to treat us. All the kids around me died, and people were surprised that I survived. The doctors told my parents that because the disease had progressed to my spinal cord I would never walk. When I started growing, I would take some steps but fall down repeatedly. I was unable to walk and basically became a cripple.

Until age seven going to school was incredibly difficult. My learning ability was impaired. What they were teaching me was very hard to grasp. The kids made fun of me and laughed at me, and I felt extremely depressed.

One day my father went to South Africa, where he met an evangelist who invited him to an event they were planning in Ghana in the near future. The evangelist prophesied to my father that he had a son who couldn't walk, and he thought that Jesus would heal him if my father would only believe.

11

He said some other very specific things about my family that he could not possibly have known. This was surprising to my father. Back then my father was heavily into politics; he was not a religious man. But at that time my condition being what it was, he was desperate so he agreed to go.

When my father told me about this man, I was very happy. I was hoping that what the man said would be true. I didn't know God at the time, but I was hoping for anything that could make me walk and make me a normal kid.

When this man came to Ghana, they held an evangelistic revival meeting in a large stadium. They invited my family, and we went, I in my wheelchair. We got there late. The place was packed with thousands of people, and we were at the back of the stadium. The man was ministering on the stage up front, and then he pointed in my direction. He said there was somebody in the back of the stadium who had meningitis and was in a wheelchair and unable to walk. There were many people in wheelchairs, so when he said that, we weren't sure he was talking about me. He repeated it and said where the person was in the stadium (pointing toward me). He described what I was wearing and my approximate age and said, "Bring him forward."

They brought me in front of the man, and he said, "Why are you sitting in that wheelchair?"

I said, "Obviously because I'm paralyzed. I can't walk and I've been like this for years."

He asked, "Do you believe that Jesus can heal you?" At that time I had no idea who Jesus was. I was looking around and there were many miracles happening—lame people walking, deaf people hearing, and blind people seeing.

I said, "If that is Jesus who is healing people, then because my eyes have seen, I would like to believe in Jesus."

He said, "Do you know you've been healed already? Get up and walk."

I rose a little bit, then fell back into my wheelchair. He said, "In the name of Jesus, get up and walk!" and he put his hand over my head. I could feel some sort of power, like heat, flow all over my body. He repeated a third time, "Get up in the name of Jesus!" and I felt a shock go through my back, like electricity—and I rose up! I began taking a few steps. I was walking for the first time in my life!

I was smiling and looking around and I said, "Wow! For all these years, if I had known Jesus when I was younger, I wouldn't have missed anything!" (At the time I was seven years old.) The man of God said, "You haven't missed anything. Jesus has healed you, and He's going to add all your wasted years to your life and bless you more." He also prophesied, "Though he couldn't walk, this boy will walk faster than those around him. He will grow up to be a prominent person in society." Then he blessed me and left.

I thought, "Wow! If this Jesus can heal me, then I want to know about this Jesus." What I'd been through was exceedingly tough. When I remember my childhood, I remember the kids making fun of me, laughing at me, telling me I was nobody, and that I would have no future. It was very hard for me. So I began to pick up my Bible and read whatever I could.

From that age until I was in high school, it was still tough for me—the healing had just taken place, and I had to get used to the fact that I had to walk after using a wheelchair for years. It took some time. It was when I was about fourteen years old that I completely regained my neurological ability to walk normally.

I began to get involved in school sports activities. I started running in the mountains and doing marathons. I ran on the 400-meter relay team and was one of the top athletes in my school. I was running much faster than the other students, and I won a lot of certificates, including two high school marathon championships. It was amazing, and I thank God that He touched my life back then.

Jesus is real. I'm from Africa—my ancestors worshipped idols, and I know what it means to worship idols. I remember that my parents took me to certain priests of these idols so that I would be healed. They couldn't heal me. I was never healed until I met Jesus. Jesus can heal—whether you are sick, deaf, blind, paralyzed, or have AIDS. My family knows—I was paralyzed. Today I can walk. Today I am a doctor, and I touch people's lives. Today I minister to people and feel the presence of God in so many ways.

All you have to do is believe in Jesus and give yourself to Him, and He will touch you. My encouragement to you is to keep your hope in Christ, for He is real, and He loves you.

In addition to being a pastor and an evangelist, **George Baah**, DPM, is a full-time podiatrist whose practice is based in New York City. He likes to say God uses him to "save souls *and* soles." For more information, write georgebaahdpm@gmail.com.

4

Jesus and the Jet Ski

With God all things are possible.
MATTHEW 19:26

MY NAME IS Fred Klemm. I was born on Long Island, New York, in 1972. Growing up, I was a terror—bad news. I was a football player and a fighter. I was rugged, mean, and nasty. I liked fights and instigated them, both verbally and physically. I married my high school sweetheart, and we had two beautiful boys, but my wife and I didn't get along well. I was filled with anger back then, and by the time I was twenty-three we were separated.

Regarding my spiritual life, when I was young (around nine or ten), I would spend the summers with my cousin, and we would attend Catholic Mass. I didn't really believe in God, and I thought if there was a God and He was as forgiving as everybody said, then He would forgive me. That's about as much thought as I gave the subject, but then something dramatic happened that changed my world.

On August 17, 1996, I was riding a Jet Ski at Smith Point Beach in Shirley, New York. I was going fast—around forty miles per hour—when I jumped a large wake from a passing fishing boat and hit a sandbar. I sustained massive head trauma from the impact and was knocked out. I floated unconscious in the water for approximately seventeen minutes until someone pulled me out.

I was flown by helicopter to the hospital, where I was put on life support. I remained comatose and wasn't expected to live through the night. To everyone's surprise, I did. The doctors told my family that I would likely not survive the next week. I lived, still comatose and on life support. I continued in this state week after week, month after month. All during

15

that time the doctors told my family that I probably would not wake up. If I did, they said I'd likely be blind, brain damaged, or paralyzed.

While all this was occurring, I remained comatose and had no idea what was happening. I thought I'd gone to sleep with my wife beside me, that my kids were asleep in the next room, and that everything was fine. Then I thought I was dreaming, but it wasn't a dream—I had a vision. I saw Jesus Christ at the Last Supper with His apostles around Him at the table. I knew who Jesus was from going to Catholic Church, but I didn't really believe in God. Yet I saw Jesus. He was wearing a white robe or a sheet. I could see His face, but I couldn't make out the details. It was vague, but I knew in my heart it was Jesus. He didn't say anything—He just got up and walked over to me. He reached out with His hand toward me, and I reached up. As He touched my hand, I instantly woke up. After being in a coma nearly six months, when Jesus touched me, I immediately awakened.

I discovered I was in a hospital bed, which I later learned was in St. John's Hospital in Smithtown, New York. But at the time I had no idea where I was or what had happened. There were machines all around me and wires all around my body. I was on life support and was so confused. I looked around the room and saw pictures of my kids on the wall and a wheelchair next to the bed. I panicked—I got really scared and started pulling the tubing out of my body. I remember one of the tubes hurt really badly coming out—it was my feeding tube.

I crawled out of bed and fell to the floor. My muscles had atrophied so much from not moving for six months that I couldn't walk. I was weak, and I crawled and weaved all around trying to catch my balance and stand, but I couldn't. I ended up leaning against the wall, then hobbling into the hallway where there was a nurses' station and some people around. It was about 2:30 a.m. As I came stumbling up to the station, the nurses started screaming and came running over to me. Everyone was shocked to see me awake. I didn't know what was going on. They brought me back to the room and started trying to stabilize me.

The road to restored health was long and difficult. I spent a full year in the hospital. I had to learn how to walk and speak again after being immobilized for six months. I had to go through physical, occupational, and speech therapy—in the hospital and on an outpatient basis after I was released.

Eventually I started telling my story about seeing Jesus and how He reached out and touched me. I don't know if they believed me or not. I probably wouldn't have believed it either because I didn't even believe in God at that time. But it happened to me—Jesus touched me, and that's when I woke up. It was a true miracle.

Since that time my life has changed for the better. For one, I definitely believe in Jesus now. I gave my life to Him and became a born-again Christian, and the Lord has blessed me abundantly. The doctors said I was supposed to be blind, mentally impaired, or paralyzed, and I have none of those conditions. They said I would need to take anti-seizure medication for the rest of my life, but I don't. I have a job, a driver's license, and my own car.

The Lord has removed the anger and has given me peace in my soul. I am so happy and thankful for all He's done for me. I didn't even believe in God, yet He reached out and saved me. When God Himself reaches out to you personally, then you really know the truth. It goes beyond religion, and nobody can ever take that away from you.

Everybody's testimony is different. I'm just telling people what I've seen and experienced. I didn't see any bright light at the end of a tunnel or anything like that. I saw Jesus Christ at the Last Supper with His apostles. I know Jesus healed me and allowed me to live so I could tell others about His goodness and mercy.

If you're having doubts about God, remember I was once like you. Take heart—there is a God, His name is Jesus Christ, and He loves you and wants to have a personal relationship with you. Ask Him to come into your heart and direct your path, and you'll see; He'll change your life for the better like He did for me.

Fred Klemm lives today on his native Long Island, New York, where he still shares his testimony of Jesus's amazing work in his life with all who will listen. For more information, write jetski106@gmail.com.

5

I Still Have a Leg to Stand On

For He shall give His angels charge over
you, to keep you in all your ways. In
their hands they shall bear you up, lest
you dash your foot against a stone.

PSALM 91:11–12

Y NAME IS Joseph Fazzina. I was born in 1933 in Boston,
Massachusetts, but have lived on Long Island, New York, for more than
forty years. I believe in God and that He has all the attributes accepted
in traditional conservative theology: omnipotence, omniscience, omni-
presence, He's all holy, etc. I also believe that Jesus is the Son of God, the
second person of the Trinity, and that He proved who He was by pre-
dicting His own ignominious death and glorious resurrection. I believe
in divine intervention and God's power to perform miracles. The incident I'm about to recount is definitely a case of divine intervention.

In the mid-1950s, I was a student at Montfort College in Litchfield,
Connecticut. The awe-inspiring campus comprised one hundred eighty
acres of prime land—a picturesque, sylvan landscape with hundreds of
trees, hiking trails, gardens, meadows for livestock, and barns for storage
of hay and the care of animals. The entire domain exuded peace, tran-
quility, and motivation to praise God for the wonder of His works.

The students were afforded the opportunity to work on the grounds
to offset some of the costs of tuition, room, and board. We worked on
Thursday afternoons and Saturdays, as well as the entire summer. Since
I didn't have much money and wasn't afraid to work (some say the latter
has changed but the former hasn't), I took advantage of the opportunities.

The administration decided to build a tourist-attraction center, replete

19

with a gift shop, auditorium, and commons. It would be a rest area where visitors could shop, attend conferences and lectures, read, pray, and take in the beauty of God's handiwork in such an invigorating and inspiring environment.

To achieve this goal much work had to be done. The designated area—about twenty acres—had to be cleared to prepare the site for the construction project. Trees had to be felled, brush and debris had to be cleared, stumps and limbs had to be cut and carted away.

My assignment was to hook one end of a heavy chain around the base of designated trees. The other end of the chain was connected to the winch of a powerful tractor. The procedure was the following: I would hook the chain to the base of a tree after the operator had backed the tractor to within five feet of the tree. Then the operator would move fast forward, tightening the chain and uprooting the tree by the force of the tractor.

There was much noise and activity all around: saws were buzzing, motors were running, axes and sledgehammers were pounding; workers were moving around, some shouting instructions. There was a cacophony of noises and shouts.

In the midst of this bustling activity, I was busy doing my work—and then it happened. As I hooked the chain around the base of one of the trees, somehow my right leg ended up between the tree trunk and the loop of the chain. Without warning, the operator moved the tractor forward since he'd already seen me hook the chain on the tree. As I saw the tractor move, my leg between the tree and chain and the chain's loop getting smaller, I froze! I couldn't speak, couldn't yell, couldn't shout. In short, I panicked!

Just as I was about to lose my leg, a supervisor standing about ten feet away somehow realized what was happening and had the presence of mind amid the din of activities and sounds to take action. I could feel the chain against my skin. The supervisor screamed at the top of his lungs, "*Stop! Stop! He's caught!*"

To this day I don't know how the operator heard the supervisor amid all the noise and distraction—amid the din, confusion, and pandemonium—or how he stopped on time. However, all of this happened and the chain stopped on my right leg just below the knee. I'm sure that were it not for divine intervention, I would have died of fright or at least have been crippled for more than fifty years.

I have no rational explanation for why I'm still physically whole and my leg wasn't severed. For me, it was definitely a case of divine intervention. It is inexplicable in human terms how all the elements came together:

1. The supervisor

2. The screams to stop

3. The split-second reaction of the operator

4. The chain not cutting off my leg

5. All this in the midst of all that noise and confusion

In reflecting on that moment, I've thanked God multiple times. I often wonder why this incident occurred, as well as several other even worse life-threatening incidents in my life, and why I was spared. I *should* have been dead several times according to the ordinary laws of nature. I realize now that my survival is only due to the merciful plan of God in my regard. God spared my life many times. Divine intervention indeed.

Maybe I was spared for this moment, to give testimony to the reality of a divine power that sustains us no matter what, until our mission is complete. I believe that everyone has a mission. For some it will last a few days, for others a long lifetime, maybe a hundred years. Perhaps I was spared to be the parent of this book's author and editor, or to influence students in my long career as an educator, or to inspire some to develop a deeper relationship with Jesus Christ, or to get someone to think about his own calling and destiny in the hereafter.

As I ponder the meaning of life, and the possible missions assigned to me by divine providence, I encourage you to think of your own place in the plan of God. Think about it, pray about it, and dwell upon the true values of life, bearing in mind that we do not have here a lasting city.

Whatever your mission, remember that Jesus Christ died for you and has called you to Himself, and you will be with Him forever after His purpose for you is completed. Until then hope in Him, trust in Him, talk to Him, thank Him for life and the privilege of being with Him where "eye has not seen, nor ear heard...the things which God has prepared for those who love Him" (1 Cor. 2:9). Isn't that something worth living for, waiting for, dying for? I submit that it is. May the Lord bless you always and love you forever.

Joseph Fazzina was born in Boston, Massachusetts, and has been an educator all his professional life. He holds a master's degree in counselor's education from St. John's University and is a college professor of romance languages. He is also an active member of Grace Lutheran Church on Long Island, New York, where he resides with Gwen, his wife of more than forty years. For more information, write fazzina@earthlink.net.

6

Walking in the Supernatural

You are my hiding place; You preserve
me from trouble; You surround
me with songs of deliverance.

PSALM 32:7, NAS

MY NAME IS Dennis Swift. I was born in New Mexico in 1952. I'd like to share several of the many divine interventions I've experienced during my long walk with Jesus Christ.

In June 1969 I gave my life to Jesus at a stadium crusade in Alamogordo, New Mexico, and received a calling to preach the gospel. I preached my first sermon at age sixteen. I studied at several colleges, earning a BA in religion and two master's degrees. I then planted a Nazarene church in California when I was twenty-six years old.

I went on to pastor several churches over the years, eventually ending up with a small congregation in Oregon. We had no church building, so initially we kept moving from location to location, then we met in a school for a while. After seven years, I prayed and fasted for twenty-one days, then contacted a real estate agent. Property out here costs $650,000 to $800,000 per acre, and I didn't see any way we could purchase anything.

Then in May 2006, a blind evangelist from South Africa named Hamilton Filmalter came to our church to preach. He told me the Lord had shown him a vision about us. He said that by the end of that year, we would have a building. It would be an unusual-looking building, like a warehouse, but it wouldn't be a warehouse.

On December 15, 2006, I received a phone call from an Argentinean evangelist named Hector Cammertoni, who didn't know I was looking

23

for a building. He said he'd been praying and the Lord told him that I wasn't going to get a church but a temple.

The same day, a Realtor e-mailed me. She sent a picture of an old-looking church building. It was far away, so I was reluctant to go see it. But I contacted the realtor anyway, and we arranged a time to look at the building.

When we arrived, I saw it was called Kesser Temple! The building had been constructed in 1888 as Emmanuel Baptist Church. But in more recent years it had become home to the only Jewish Orthodox temple in the city, and the congregation was moving.

The congregation was having an open house, and many people from churches, museums, and real estate companies were looking at the property. I bid $510,000, but the building was probably worth $1.5 million.

The bidding time passed, and then early in the morning of December 24, on Christmas Eve, I had a vision from the Lord in which I saw angels going in and out of that building. They said to me, "Come get it. It's yours."

The next day, Christmas 2006, I got an e-mail that read: "You don't know me, but I'm the principal owner of the building. I met all the prospective buyers at the open house. We're making the decision on to whom we'll sell the building, not based on price, but upon who we think should get the building. We'd like to sell you the building for $510,000." That was an amazing Christmas gift and truly a divine intervention!

That's just one story of God's intervention in my life. Through that experience, I realized that you don't need for everybody to like you; you only need *the right person* to like you. One day of favor is worth a thousand days of labor! You just have to serve God and watch Him do things and move in your life!

I do archaeological studies in the Nazca area of Peru, and I've had several incidents of divine intervention there as well. In 2007 I was headed into Nazca with some people, and I had a vision. It was black and dark. This is a cursed area of the world; it's rife with shamanism and spiritism, and the people are very poor. In this vision, it looked as if the firmament of heaven was black. There were zipperlike openings in the sky, and angels were coming down through them to the earth and visiting people.

Later I was in my hotel room in Nazca, just before bedtime, and I had a very frightening experience. I saw a demon, or some kind of spirit, put a snakelike mark over my heart. I didn't understand it, but I knew it was something evil and dangerous and that I'd been marked in some way. I knew something evil was going to happen. It was very real and scary.

The next day as we were eating lunch with fellow creation scientist Carl Baugh and some of our friends at their home in Nazca, I started choking. Amazingly, Dr. Baugh had lost two friends in separate incidents before who had choked to death under similar circumstances. I didn't even have a big piece of meat in my mouth. What I'd been eating was very small, a minor thing, but I just couldn't seem to clear my throat. I went outside to try and get some fresh air but just couldn't catch my breath and kept choking.

A missionary was there who was a nurse. At her recommendation I tried changing positions, drinking water, even lying down and lowering my head over the side of a bed. This episode lasted more than an hour, and during the entire time, my wife, Dr. Baugh, and our friends were praying for me. Eventually I got through it. It turned out I was choking on one small grain of rice. I believe that was not a coincidence but a spiritual attack. I thank God that through the prayers I was able to survive.

Finally, I went back and enjoyed the rest of the meal with our host family. As we talked, the members of the family, who had known me for years, kept saying that every time I came for a visit they could feel God's presence, and that they knew God was real. That night, the wife, her husband, and their son all accepted Christ. Then the husband (who is not a man given to believing in the miraculous) told everyone that when we started praying, he saw two angels come into his house. Because of this incident, nearly one hundred people accepted Christ into their lives in that shantytown within two months! Now we kind of have a ministry there in the shantytowns, and I go there to minister once or twice a year.

If you're struggling with doubt about God, I would encourage you to put your faith in Jesus Christ today and in so doing enter a relationship with the God who created you and loves you. People need to hear about miracles. Without the supernatural, Christianity is merely a religious book club. You take out the supernatural, and there's nothing left of Christianity. Jesus is real, and His power is real. I pray He becomes real in your life.

Dennis Swift, PhD, is an archaeolo-
gist, adventurer, and author, as well as
a pastor, lecturer, and creation science
researcher. He travels to distant lands
a few times each year to work with
local people and institutions, carefully
recording the existence of interesting
artifacts that corroborate the Bible's
history, particularly as they relate to
the coexistence of dinosaurs and humans, as taught in the Bible.
For more information, write drdino1@hotmail.com or visit
www.dinosaursandman.com or www.dinosaursandhumans.org.

7

Raised From the Dead

Why should it be thought incredible
by you that God raises the dead?
ACTS 26:8

*M*Y NAME IS Mark Excel. I'm a missionary, and God has done amazing miracles in my life. I hope my testimony encourages you.

I was born in 1956 to a preacher and deaconess in Nigeria, Africa. I had a good background and education, and I loved the Lord from my childhood. As a boy I became born again and Holy Spirit filled after watching the *Jesus* film. Life was wonderful until the civil war started in 1967. Biafra, in southeastern Nigeria where I lived, rebelled against the government, and war waged for three years. Soldiers took over Biafra, and thousands of people died. I became a sickly, malnourished refugee. I witnessed shelling and killing. Bombs killed people in my presence and buried us in the ground. My parents and I were fortunate to survive; the Lord was with us.

After the war I put myself through elementary and high school. I then moved to Lagos and attended secondary school, earning my accounting degree. While attending school I worked as an account clerk.

I married in 1986 and started a ministry. My wife, Ann, and I bought land and built the Voice of Freedom Bible Church. We taught the Bible, and the church grew and thrived.

The Lord then started telling me to quit my job. I was resistant to this idea. He kept saying I had to resign, even leave the church I founded, and go out as a missionary. I told my wife, "This cannot be possible. God knows how much I've suffered since childhood and what I've lived through. I'm married now. I must settle down and take care of you and the kids."

27

The voice kept speaking, and the burden increased, until September 10, 1989. That day's experience revolutionized my life. On that fateful Sunday, I preached at church. We returned home and had a nice time—but during the night while we slept, something happened.

On Monday morning Ann awoke to my dead body lying on the bed next to her! I had died during the night!

What had happened?

That night Jesus came to me. He walked into the room and said, "Come with Me. I'm taking you to the land of the dead, that you might see what is happening." I quickly realized what He meant—I was going to die. I started crying. I couldn't object to following Him; the power was so strong. I followed Him through what seemed like a tunnel.

In Africa we have a custom: if something bad happens, people put their hands on their head and walk on the street. Whether they are crying or not, you'll know something is wrong. I walked with my hands on my head, crying, following the Lord.

He turned and asked me, "As you are coming, can you go back and take your money?"

"No," I said.

"Can you get your wife and child?"

"No."

He said, "This is the lonely road everyone will walk. When you walk this road, you cannot take anything with you from this life. That is why I asked you to go preach the gospel, but you disobeyed Me." I continued crying as I followed Him. He was taking me to the land of the dead. In short, I thought I *was* dead.

When we reached the tunnel's end, a gate opened, we passed through, and it closed. We turned a corner to the left, and there was another gate with angels on either side. Jesus didn't speak. They seemed to communicate with their eyes. The angels opened the gate, and we were in hellfire.

The angels sat by the gate. Every second I saw somebody being pushed into hell, screaming, "Oh, my God! Is this where I come?" Especially those who used to attend church but didn't repent. The hell I saw resembled a factory. There were machines producing heat and shooting out flames. Everyone stood at attention; fire came out from the machines and burned them. The people cried but didn't die. They were screaming, "Water! Water!" Their faces were disfigured, like when fire burns someone and the skin peels off. They were really tormented. We were by the gate watching, and they could see us. The flames didn't breach the barrier; we were close to them but didn't receive any heat. How that happened, I don't know.

Everyone was crying, and Jesus said, "Have you seen this?" I broke down. I couldn't stand seeing how people were suffering. He said, "Come." He took me and turned again to the left. Another gate opened and there was a bigger place. More torment. Another group was there, as if inside a huge factory, and people were still being brought and packed in.

Nobody could say anything but shout, "Water!" They looked up and saw the Lord. It seemed as if they were about to worship Him, in a type of begging or pleading. I saw remorse and repentance in them. I was reminded of a Bible passage that says, "God also has highly exalted Him and given Him the name which is above every name, that at the name of Jesus every knee should bow" (Phil. 2:9–10).

The Lord said, "These people are seeking repentance, but it is too late. Those who refused to worship Me in life will worship Me in hell." I was seriously weeping. It was horrible.

He took me to a third gate. When it opened, it was horrifying. I saw a schoolmate who used to sit with me in elementary school. He was killed during the war. I know his family. He called my name, "Mark! Go tell my family where I am! They made me to be here!" I collapsed, weeping bitterly. I couldn't walk or do anything.

The Lord said, "Have you seen this? This is what is happening." As He was talking, people were trooping in. The Lord raised me up and said, "Come. I'll show you another mystery." We went up a crooked, narrow road. Leaving hell, a gate opened and we burst into an open place—heaven.

This place looked like everything was made of gold. He took me from room to room, and what I saw weren't walls but something almost transparent, yet reflective like a mirror. While you're walking, you see yourself coming, but when you reach the wall, it parts and you enter another room. You would never find the way out without somebody leading you.

I saw people I'd never met, but it was as if I'd known them all my life. People were embracing, congratulating, and welcoming each other.

Everyone was in the mode of worship. The angels played many different trumpets, and the music was incredible—otherworldly. I even saw what looked like construction, as if mansions with great rooms were being built.

Then the Lord said, "Have you seen the two mysteries? Go tell the world what you've seen. I send you as My ambassador."

I wanted to say, "No, Lord, I want to remain here."

Before I could speak, the gate was opened and I was outside the gate. I heard a voice say, "Here, we only take instructions. We don't argue." Then the gate closed, and I opened my eyes in my room.

I didn't know it was already afternoon and they had called an ambulance to take me to the mortuary because I had been pronounced dead. God sent two men to my house. One of them, Pastor Olufemi, is still my friend to this day. God directed them to come and stop anyone from moving my body.

When my wife awoke and discovered my body, she started screaming. Neighbors heard her cries and came and took her to a neighbor's house nearby. The two men of God and other church members went there that morning, praying and prophesying over my dead body for hours—from morning until afternoon. At around 1:00 p.m. I began breathing and moving my fingers.

When they saw that they said, "He's breathing!" They arranged for the ambulance to take me to a clinic run by the wife of one of the men who came to pray for me. I spent eight days in the hospital, in and out of consciousness. Finally on the eighth day I awoke and saw my wife next to the bed.

"What are we doing here?" I asked.

She exclaimed, "You were dead and now you're back!"

"There's nothing wrong with me," I said. "Let's go home."

I looked at the many IVs in my hands and body. I tried pulling them out, and my wife said, "Hold on! Let me get the doctor."

She called the doctor, but I said, "I want to go home." They tested me repeatedly but couldn't find anything wrong. They removed the IVs one by one, observed me for several hours, and finally discharged me. I was OK, except that I couldn't walk. I had to learn to walk again, like a baby.

After that experience I answered God's call. The Lord eventually sent me as a missionary to Togo, then to America.

One thing I must say very clearly. After the Lord shut the gate behind me and said, "Tell the world what you've seen," He then said, "Many will believe you, and many will not, but do what I asked you to do."

Few have come to believe, but I'm doing what God called me to do. The one thing that sustains me is that lonely road I walked with the Lord. It was that experience—when He turned back and asked, "Can you go back and get your money? Or your wife and child?" and I said no—that has sustained me all the days of my ministry. That experience changed my life. I'm sure anyone who has been to hell and seen people wailing and crying for water, and also has seen the glory of heaven—I don't think that person could be a normal human being again.

Immediately after my experience I was paralyzed and couldn't walk. I had to learn to walk anew. That experience represents my new walk in the Lord. It's transformed me into a new man. I used to be very proud and arrogant. After that experience, I was utterly broken. Today I remain quiet and peaceful. I mind my business and do what God called me to do. I don't argue. Those who are meant to believe will believe. Praise God, and thank you for reading my testimony.

Mark Excel is a church planter and apostolic minister who focuses on missions, global evangelism, revival, and deliverance. He and his wife, Ann, are co-hosts of the TV program *Moment of Freedom*. Mark also holds a doctorate in theology. He and his wife are blessed with six children and live on Long Island, New York. For more information, write missionaryexcel@aol.com.

8

Shot Forty-Three Times

We also glory in tribulations, knowing that
tribulation produces perseverance; and
perseverance, character; and character, hope.
Now hope does not disappoint, because the
love of God has been poured out in our hearts.

ROMANS 5:3–5

Y NAME IS Derrick Holmes. I was born in 1958 and raised
in a musical family in Los Angeles, California. I always believed in God,
but I didn't always listen to His voice, which will become evident as I
share my story.

My parents inspired me to pursue a music career. I began piano lessons at age eight. By high school I was proficient in writing, arranging,
and recording music, and I ultimately became a busy musician. After
high school I made a good living in music until 1980. With the advent
of disco, people stopped paying for ten-piece bands. They'd hire a DJ
for much less than a band costs, so I couldn't make a living performing
anymore. I put my music career on hold and worked as a bus dispatcher.

By 1986 I'd worked my way up to division manager for a major transportation company. I'd also married and had a daughter. Juggling a
demanding management job, a new family, and doing as many music gigs
as possible to try to restart my music career proved to be overwhelming.
As a way to cope with my responsibilities, I made a bad choice. I turned
to drugs.

I would say it was "recreational," but it began consuming my life. I
thought I could stop anytime and that it wouldn't get the best of me, but
I couldn't perform at work after being up all night. I started showing

up late, and I couldn't keep it together, so I lost my job. I was having trouble at home because I was never there, and my wife and I separated. I ended up homeless, living in my car in Hollywood. My daily agenda was to hustle money all day to buy drugs at night, then sit in my car and use them.

It was a downward spiral, and I wasn't taking care of any responsibilities. My car's registration tags were expired, and after numerous warnings by police, my car was impounded.

I was too embarrassed to go to family or friends. I tried staying with associates from the streets, sleeping anywhere I could. It was total insanity, with people going back and forth for drugs—nobody sleeping or working.

I always believed in God. And this may sound strange, but while all this was happening I was praying and trying to hide what I was doing from Him, as if that were possible. I was constantly praying, "Protect me. Protect my family and everyone around me." I was going against His will with the drugs, but He guided me out nonetheless.

That was my life until everything came to a head on September 16, 1994. While I was trying to buy drugs that night, a fight broke out between a teenage drug dealer and one of his customers. As I stood watching, the dealer drew a knife and stabbed his customer. The bloodied victim took off running, and the dealer nonchalantly turned to me and asked, "How much do you need?"

I couldn't believe what had just happened. Suddenly I didn't want the drugs. The Lord told me to leave, and I started walking away and praying. I walked back to my car (which I'd just gotten back from the impounding), but I didn't get in. Instead I walked all night from Hollywood to mid-city Los Angeles, entered a police station, and turned myself in. By then I'd been arrested multiple times and had violated my probation. There were several warrants out for me.

Instead of accepting my surrender, the probation officer said, "Going to jail won't help you." He told me to go to the Delaney Street Foundation, a two-year drug rehabilitation program. I entered on September 17, 1994. While in Delaney Street I continued praying to be able to get my life back on track. I never gave up, no matter how hard it got. I knew God had sent me to Delaney Street, and I wasn't going to leave until I completed my two-year commitment and was sure my faith and mind-set were strong enough to never go back to drugs.

Thank God, I got clean, graduating from the program in 1996. I eventually found work as a limousine driver and reconciled with my wife and daughter. Things were looking up, until one fateful night in January 1998, when my life changed forever.

I'd finished my shift at about 12:30 a.m., parked the limo, got my car, and headed home. I exited the Hollywood Freeway and headed south. As I crossed Santa Monica Boulevard, my engine died. I walked to a bus stop to get a ride home, where I happened to meet an old friend. As we were talking, waiting for the bus, I noticed a young man running toward us. It appeared he was fleeing from someone or something.

Shortly after he reached us, I heard multiple gunshots, and watched the man's lifeless body fall to the ground, half of his head blown off. At the same time, my friend and I were also hit with gunfire. My friend made it to the pay phone and called 911. I was on the ground being shot, and they also shot up the phone. I remember the aluminum from the phone going into my friend's face before she hit the ground. I saw muzzle flashes as I lay in the street being shot again and again.

I didn't know what this shooting was about, but I had no doubt I was going to die. I began saying my prayers and asking for forgiveness for everything I'd done. Right when I said, "Amen," the ground started shaking. I thought it was the end, but it was actually a fire truck that pulled up next to me, blocking the bullets.

I awoke in the ICU of Cedars-Sinai Medical Center two days later, where I was informed that I'd undergone more than twelve hours of surgery after having been shot forty-three times in a gang-related drive-by shooting. I was hit by forty 9mm rounds and three 12-gauge shotgun blasts, which took off my left leg below the knee.

To survive after being shot that many times had to be a miracle. I think it's safe to say God intervened. He wasn't through with me yet.

I spent eleven months in the hospital, plus six months in a convalescent home for rehabilitation to relearn how to walk. Every day I thank God for sparing my life. Throughout the ordeal, I questioned why that happened to me. I think it has been to show people that if God has a plan for your life, nothing will get in the way of its completion.

I wanted to share my testimony to let people know that God is great, and whatever you do you've got to include Jesus in it. Stay strong in faith, don't give up, and by God's grace you'll overcome, prevail, and move on!

Derrick Holmes continues to stay strong in his faith, encouraging people with his testimony and letting them know that God has a purpose for their lives. He and his wife live in Los Angeles, California, and have a daughter and a grandson. For more information, write derrickholmes59@yahoo.com. To view medical documentation, see Appendix.

9

The Christian Car Guy

There is no fear in love; but perfect
love casts out fear....He who fears
has not been made perfect in love.

1 JOHN 4:18

*M*Y NAME IS Robby Dilmore. I was born in 1955 in Idaho,
but moved frequently growing up, as my dad worked for the auto
industry and was often transferred to different cities. I started working
in car dealerships in 1971, and by 1998 I was dealer principle of a Chrysler
Dodge Jeep store in Winston-Salem, North Carolina. That's where I was
when God called me to start the *Christian Car Guy* radio show in 2006.

I wasn't raised in a churchgoing home. I was already married with
children when I gave my life to Jesus. I'd been reading Norman Vincent
Peale's *The Power of Positive Thinking*. In his book Peale says that if you
want to develop a positive mental attitude, get up an hour early every day
and read the Bible. So I did, thinking it would help me sell more cars.
From reading the Bible and attending a class at a local church with my
wife, I eventually understood that I was a sinner and needed a Savior.

I seemed to have been born with fears I couldn't understand. Until
1995, one of the worst was my fear of the dark. You wouldn't think it,
since I was six feet five inches tall and weighed two hundred fifty pounds.
But my wife will tell you that for years if I heard a noise downstairs I'd
send her to investigate. You'd find me hiding under the covers on many
dark nights. Something had me creeped out. I didn't know what, but I
was petrified.

One night everything came to a head. My wife was away and we lived
in a dark, creepy old house. There was a lightning storm outside, and I

was terrified. Having just begun my walk with Christ, I'd heard we were supposed to lay our fears at His feet. I was more than ready to oblige.

I prayed, "Lord, I don't know how, but I'd really like to give You this fear."

Surprisingly God answered me (which scared me even more). "Robby, what's the worst that could happen?" He asked.

"Someone could walk in here with a knife and *whack, thump, bash, gouge!*" I said.

Then God said words that changed my life: "Robby, what would be so bad about that?"

For the first time I thought about my own death as a Christian, realizing I would get to see His face. I'd never thought that "to die is gain" (Phil. 1:21). Although I didn't suddenly lose that fear, I was able to sleep that night, and the healing began. Like the Bible says, "Perfect love drives out fear" (1 John 4:18, NIV). Over the next few years I grew and was healed. It's been years since it bothered me. That understanding of my own mortality was a critical life lesson God had for me.

A year later I needed that insight. I'd been getting sores on my body. It quickly went from a few sores to dozens. They didn't hurt, but they rose up, flat and red, from beneath my skin. My wife insisted I go to the dermatologist, who took a biopsy.

When the doctor's office called several days later, it was a conversation I will never forget. "Mr. Dilmore, we need you to come to the office to get your test results," the nurse said.

With my puffed up view of my position in life I responded, "I'm very busy. I have a dealership to run here. You can give me the results over the phone. I'm a big boy."

"Mr. Dilmore, you have lymphoma," she said calmly.

My response is almost comical now. "What's lymphoma?"

"It's cancer of the lymphatic system."

"I'll be right there." Suddenly my position changed. I had time to see any doctor they needed me to see.

This began a crazy journey any cancer survivor understands: phone calls, life and death discussions with loved ones, all sorts of tests and waiting—waiting on results, on another treatment, on another test to see if that treatment helped. I gained a clear understanding of why they call you a "patient."

My sister worked at the University of Michigan hospital. I sent her my pathology report. The diagnosis was non-Hodgkin's angiocentric cutaneous T-cell lymphoma. When my sister said that was sometimes known as extranodal natural killer T-cell lymphoma (a very rare disease), and the few cases in the United States had no survivors over several months, my mind returned to the lesson in the dark, creepy house.

"What's the worst that can happen?" I recalled.

That may be hard to understand, but it was truly my mind-set. Yes, my wife and family were heavy on my mind, but I would get to see Jesus.

As for the faith to be healed, it wasn't the case with me. Although many folks were praying for me and bringing me all kinds of concoctions, I was settled on the chemotherapy treatment my oncologist recommended. But God had other plans, that's for sure.

The Friday before I was to receive my first chemo treatment, a white-haired man, Reverend Richard Little, came into the dealership where I worked. He was acquainted with Joe Valls, my finance manager, because Joe attended his church, Reynolda Presbyterian. He walked up to Joe and announced: "The Lord told me that someone at Bob Neil Chrysler needs healing. I've come to lay hands on them and anoint them with oil."

Joe responded, "It must be Robby Dilmore. He has a deadly form of cancer."

Again I'll say, not only did I not have the faith to be healed, but I also was clueless about the "anoint with oil and lay hands on" practice in Scripture. Honestly, I thought it was weird and certainly had no expectation of receiving an actual healing from it. I thought it couldn't hurt, however, so I went through with it. I did feel something spiritual in the process and got up with a different expectation, but I couldn't put my finger on it.

Many folks were praying, and I won't know this side of heaven exactly what did it, but God knows. What I do know is that on Friday I was covered with thick, round, red tumors, and on Monday morning when I went to the oncologist for my first treatment they were gone! Never to return, as a matter of fact. Here we are, more than sixteen years later. No tumors.

The doctor still wanted me to undergo chemotherapy, and I did. They biopsied one of the tumor scars, and when that pathology report came back the doctor said the cancer cells had changed and actually had cannibalized themselves. That was way over my head for sure. I didn't even know lymphoma was cancer at the onset of the ordeal. One thing I can testify to: God is in control of cancer.

So who's "the guy with the knife" in your life? What's your biggest fear? When you trust in Jesus, what's the worst that can happen?

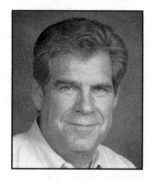
Robby Dilmore is the host of *Christian Car Guy*, a nationally syndicated radio show, and the host and producer of several other radio programs. His website, www.christiancarguy.com, provides godly counsel through hundreds of articles on everything from ways to save gas to the way to become a Christian. Robby and his wife and four children live in Winston-Salem, North Carolina. For more information, write rdilmore@WTRU.com or visit www.christiancarguy.com.

10

A Wing and a Prayer

And whatever you ask in My name, that I will
do, that the Father may be glorified in the Son.

JOHN 14:13

MY NAME IS Jean Kelly Nolting. I come from a beautiful
country called England. I've been in America for many years, and I'm
very pleased to be a citizen. I've had many experiences in my life of what
God has done, starting from when I was quite young.

I was born in 1936 and grew up in England during the Second World
War. I experienced the bombs from German planes dropping around us,
and as many children were, I was sent to a boarding school when I was
about seven years old. I spent all my school years in a girls' boarding
school, which was quite difficult and not pleasant. I was very sad to be
separated from my family. I missed them terribly, and I had a hard time
growing up in boarding school.

One of the great delights while I was there, however, was that we
attended a church that had a wonderful priest. He was a great preacher;
but not only that, he also took care of us, loved us, and was interested in
everything we did, including watching me play hockey. He also told me
about the love of Jesus Christ, which I really wasn't familiar with.

When I was about fourteen and was being confirmed, I decided to
follow Jesus for the rest of my life. I wanted Him to be part of my life,
and it changed my life completely. I came to know what it was to have a
relationship with Jesus Christ, and through that relationship I grew and
became close to Him. He became a friend of mine, and is to this day.
Having Him in my life gave me such deep peace and joy, even through
some of the very hard times in my life. Beginning with that time, I began

to see the wonderful things God does in people's lives, and how He touches lives.

One such incident that bears repeating happened around 1998. I worked for several years for an organization called Alpha, which produces a course in basic Christianity. Alpha started in London many years ago and now is being taught in nearly every country in the world. What God is doing through Alpha is exciting. I've had the privilege of traveling in America, presenting conferences and telling people about this wonderful organization. I've had to fly often because of the travel it has required to conduct these Alpha conferences.

One day I was flying to Minneapolis with a young friend from England who was helping me. Our plane had been delayed for hours, and we eventually got off the ground in New York at about nine o'clock at night. We had a full tank of fuel and made good time. When we reached Minneapolis, we could see the city lights, but eventually noticed that for about the last thirty minutes we'd been circling the airport.

I said to my friend, "Have you noticed we're not landing?"

"Yeah, I did," he said. "I wonder what's wrong."

It was a beautiful night. The sky was clear, and it was around eleven o'clock. The plane continued to circle for quite a while.

Eventually the pilot spoke on the intercom and said, "We're having trouble landing, because the flaps won't go down."

He continued, "When the flaps don't go down, we don't land. We can't land."

And that was it—he said nothing else. There was dead silence. Everybody sat there, gripping their seats and thinking, "So, what's going to happen? We go around and around until we run out of gas?"

After about another hour we were still circling, but we heard nothing from the cockpit. I think the thing that made us more frightened was that the flight attendants were nervously gripping their seats.

"Let's pray!" I said to my friend.

The woman next to me said, "Let me pray with you!" So we all held hands and started praying. As we prayed, my friend got more and more panicky, as did the lady on my right. The three of us were holding hands tightly, praying out loud, and my friend started to confess everything he'd ever done. The other woman was weeping, and we recognized that everybody was in a very deep fear, so we continued praying. We started asking for wisdom for the pilots and that the flaps would work.

Nothing. We kept circling. As we prayed, I remembered that the Bible tells us that one of the most potent prayers is that we are able to "command" things to happen in the name of Jesus.

So I held out my hand toward the wing of the plane and started praying, "Lord Jesus, I command in Your name that these flaps start to work—that they will start working and we will be able to land. In the name of Jesus."

Well, within a very short time after praying that prayer, we recognized that we were beginning to land. Slowly we came down. Nothing was said from the cockpit at any point. It was a very scary situation to be in. But you know, as I prayed and asked in the name of Jesus, I could command those flaps to come down.

We landed safely. There was great relief and joy in the cabin. After all the fear, people were just so relieved to be on the ground at last, and we praised God and thanked Him for bringing us down safely. We'd prayed very loudly, so people on the plane knew we were praying, and many spoke to us afterward.

I believe when we're in the midst of difficult times, in all types of situations, we can turn to God. We can say, "God, You are our Savior. You are the One who can help us, and we trust You now." In the middle of the tension and panic, we find rest in God because we know He is the God of the universe and all things are possible with Him (Matt. 19:26). Nothing can happen without Him. So as we prayed in that place where God was, we received a wonderful answer to our prayer, and we were able to land.

To me, this incident of divine intervention was an example of how God sometimes allows scary things in our lives just to show us how powerful He is—and how faithful He is when He delivers us from them. Amen!

After a long career in ministry and service that involved traveling and speaking all over the world, **Jean Nolting** now resides with her family in Connecticut. Jean can be contacted through her daughter, Wendy Cozzens, at wendycozzens@hotmail.com.

11

Jesus and the Jewish Atheist

For the message of the cross is foolishness
to those who are perishing, but to us who
are being saved it is the power of God.

1 CORINTHIANS 1:18

MY NAME IS Jeffrey D. Miller. I was born into a Jewish family in Pennsylvania in 1947. In my home Judaism was more a culture than a religion. I attended synagogue and Hebrew school, but my parents didn't talk about "the Big Guy in the sky," and we certainly didn't discuss Jesus. We did talk plenty about being Jewish, however. I found being Jewish without God to be empty.

By age twelve I was a thinker. I analyzed God into my teens and twenties, becoming an atheist and remaining one for twenty-four years. During that time I became increasingly confident that there was no God. By high school I crusaded against Jesus. I believed the big bang theory—life's an accident and after that, who cares? You live, you die, it's over. There's no heaven, no hell. Living and dying is all there is, and those people of faith would one day wake up and discover I'm right.

Life was all about me. I was a TV news anchor, a radio and TV talk-show host, and assistant to my city's mayor. I was a big shot, loved my wonderful life, and loved me. I didn't smoke, use drugs, or drink. I was a happy camper, not sad or depressed. I was terrific! My father was a doctor, and we were Jewish. What could be better? I'd say, "Even if there is a God, I don't need Him."

How God got hold of me involves a dramatic divine intervention. As I mentioned, I was very happy being in the public eye. I used to sign autographs, and people were excited to meet me. I didn't think I'd ever sinned in my whole life because I was such a good person. But I was a run-around bachelor in the worst sense of the word. Women were my life. I worked at a TV station and sat next to a good-looking blonde. I didn't know she was a born-again Christian, but I sure was attracted to her.

After working together a year, we started dating. We were the "odd couple": a Christian and an atheist Jew. She went before the Lord after we started dating and asked, "What have I done? How did I get mixed up with an atheist Jew?"

God spoke to her, saying that I, an atheist Jew, would come to know Jesus. I, the run-around bachelor, would marry her. Praise God, she had the wisdom not to tell me this.

She witnessed to me about Jesus and prayed continually over the two years we dated. It was like she had the tiger by the tail. I'd break dates with her to see other women, believing she'd forgive me because she was a Christian. We separated several times. I'd keep coming back. I'm sure that without her faith, she would have been long gone. She stood on God's promise and believed for my salvation, saying, "God, I know what You told me."

After two years I challenged her. I'm a journalist—rational, analytical, and logical. I'd already observed the universe, and from my vantage point there was no God in it. So I told her, "I'm sick of you telling me about God. I'm sure there's no God, and I'll prove it. I'll search for God, and when I don't find Him, you'll know once and for all that I'm right and you're wrong."

I thought it would take ten days, maximum, to prove that God doesn't exist, because I was brilliant and understood how the universe worked. Six weeks later I was still searching for God, not finding anything but wondering about a physical problem that had bothered me all my adult life; I was now in my midthirties. During those six weeks, I read every book she gave me, and prayed an empty prayer, "I know You're not there, but just in case, I'm doing everything she told me."

While reading those books, my heart didn't change. What changed was this physical problem—it wasn't there anymore. It was a digestive issue I'd had for about fifteen years. I started eating foods that normally would have bothered me, and they didn't anymore—it just went away. I said, "Hey, I lucked out. Body chemistry changes."

After six weeks of searching, I was reading a book by Disney actor Dean Jones (known for the "Herbie" films of the sixties and seventies, such as *The Love Bug)*. He was world famous, filthy rich, had everything a man could want, and was miserable. His book was about how he came to know Jesus. Normally I wouldn't even touch a book like that, but I was proving there was no God.

So I was reading his book, and he was talking about how God is real. I actually talked to the book out loud and said, "Dean, how could you be so stupid?" It was a Saturday night in July 1983; I was working a late-night weekend shift at a radio station. I was on the air, the music was playing, the microphone was off, and I was reading about how Jones's girlfriend received prayer for a physical problem and the Lord healed her.

"Who'd believe that nonsense?" I thought. "Mind over matter, maybe. But healed by a God who doesn't exist? *Baloney!*"

I had the most non-faith ever. Jesus-*schmeezus*. Who cared? I didn't think Jesus ever lived. I believed in me, in evolution, and when you die it's over.

Then I read these simple words: *"Don't you see, God healed me?"* Those words struck me. I felt something—it hit me hard. It didn't hurt, but it ran from the top of my head to the soles of my feet, up and down my body, like being on a roller coaster from the highest height.

The next thing I knew, I was crying uncontrollably. Then, on their own, my hands lifted up. I was standing in that radio studio, looking at the ceiling, hands raised, and then this atheist said, "Lord God, I'm healed!" I could barely talk because I was crying. Then this atheist Jew said, "Thank You, Jesus!" I was shocked! I couldn't believe what I was saying, but there I stood in God's presence praising His name when moments before I'd never acknowledged that He ever lived.

I got home that morning and fell on my knees. This thirty-six-year-old atheist who thought he'd never sinned said, "Lord, I'm a sinner—please forgive me. Jesus, I want You in my life. I give You my heart." I'd never been to church or read the Bible—I avoided both like the plague. Yet I was on my knees proclaiming Jesus.

From then on, my life was totally changed. I eventually grew in faith and knowledge of God's Word, became an evangelist and minister, and married my born-again Christian girlfriend, just as God had told her years before would happen. God is good, and still intervenes today—even in the lives of Jewish atheists!

Jeffrey D. Miller is a full-time traveling evangelist who has ministered in churches and messianic congregations across the country for more than twenty-three years. His vision to see Jewish people come to know Yeshua, the Messiah, is being fulfilled before his eyes. His ministry and message are also featured on *Messianic Minutes*, a radio show heard on hundreds of Christian stations nationwide. For more information, write jdmessianic@aol.com or visit www.jeffreydmiller.com.

12

The One True God Among Many

You will seek the LORD your God, and
you will find Him if you seek Him with
all your heart and with all your soul.

DEUTERONOMY 4:29

MY NAME IS Govind Sathiya Seelan. I would like to share how God intervened in my life and led me to the knowledge of and faith in Jesus Christ. I was born in 1956 in Kanchi, Madras, in South India. I was raised in a royal Hindu priesthood family. My grandfather was the Hindu priest and leader. My father died when I was a child, so my grandfather raised me and trained me to become a Hindu priest after him. Growing up, I was in the temple whenever I wasn't in school. For fifteen years I learned the Hindu Vedas and memorized Hindu scriptures. I learned how to do sacrifices, pray to the gods, and say the mantras, sutras, and more. I studied many Hindu-god stories and histories.

Hindus believe there are millions of gods. They believe nature is god. They believe living and dead people are god. They believe everything and everybody is god. They also believe in seven incarnations, that man must be born seven times in order to go to heaven. That's what I was taught and what I believed.

I went to the Hindu temple and prayed; I gave different kinds of sacrifices and did all the mantras and rituals, yet I didn't have satisfaction or happiness in my heart. I was sincerely seeking. When I bowed before the Hindu gods and prayed to them, those gods never spoke with me. They never moved. I brought sacrifices, but they never took them.

When I asked my grandfather why they never moved or spoke to me, he said, "You cannot ask those things. Just follow the tradition." Deep in my heart, I really wanted to speak with God and see Him because I believed God gave me life, eyes to see with, and a mouth to speak with.

For three years—from ages fifteen to seventeen—I honestly sought, read the Hindu scriptures, spent all my time in the temple, and listened to my grandfather and the other Hindu priests who visited the temple.

I asked everyone, "Did you see God? Did you speak with God?"

They said, "No, we cannot see Him."

Everybody had the same story. I was confused. Then I thought that maybe there is no God. Yet in my heart I had unanswered questions. I would see the stars; I would see the sun rising every day in the morning and at the right time setting in the evening.

I asked, "Why does it come at the right time? Who changes the direction of the wind? I know there is somebody behind all these things, but I don't know who He is." So I stopped praying to God in the Hindu names. I started praying only to "God."

"O God, who created the heaven and earth, who gives life to every human, please, I want to speak to You. If there is a God, please reveal Yourself. I want to see You." I started crying, reading more Hindu scriptures, spending all my time in the temple, seeking and seeking, and still nothing happened. There was no satisfaction in what I was reading.

It was in this state of dissatisfaction and desperation when on the afternoon of January 12, 1973, I went and sat in a lonely garden. I looked into the sky and cried to God, "Please, if there is a God, I want to see You!"

When I cried out, suddenly there was a great light shining in front of me, a light brighter than the sunlight. Within the light I saw a person, like a dead man hanging on a tree. When I saw this, I was so frightened that I fell down. Deep in my heart I believed that when I saw God, He would be like a Hindu god, having the golden crown and arms, and He would speak to me with Hindu words. This was entirely different. I couldn't understand it. I was so frightened, and still the light was shining, and someone was speaking to me. I didn't understand the language but in my heart I knew it meant something. I wanted to run, but I couldn't. This shining light and vision lasted about five minutes.

When the light disappeared and the sound stopped, I jumped up, ran back home, and cried out to my family, "I saw something in the sky!

I saw a light, and a person hanging on a tree like a dead man spoke to me! Please tell me who He is and what it was!"

None of my Hindu family understood what had happened to me. In fact, they thought I'd gone mad. You have to understand, at that point in my life I didn't know anything about Jesus Christ. I had never met a Christian. I had never read the Bible. I had never been to a church. I didn't know anything about Christianity. Yet I saw a dead man hanging on a tree. I asked everyone I met who the man in my vision was. Nobody from my village had any clue.

Three months later I met a man from another village who gave me a book. I didn't realize it at the time, but by the grace of God, it was a Bible. I opened the book, not knowing it was a Bible, to 1 Peter chapter 2. I looked at just two verses. Verse 24 was flashing before my eyes. It said He came to this world to take away all our sins and infirmities "in His body on the tree." When I read, "He bore our sins in His own body *on the tree*" (emphasis added), I was shocked! That's what I saw in the light—a man hanging on a tree like a dead man! Now I was reading in this book of the man who died on the tree!

I eventually learned that Peter was speaking of Jesus Christ, the Son of the one true God. I renounced idol worship and committed my life to Him. It wasn't easy. I was disowned by my family, beaten many times, and cast out of my village, but I was happy. I had found the truth. I later went on to seminary and became a pastor and an evangelist. In my many years of ministry I have established more than one thousand churches and baptized more than a half-million converts. Many years after my conversion I even had the honor of leading my family and entire village of five hundred people to Christ.

The Bible never tells a lie. What God said was happening two thousand years ago is happening today in my life. Jesus Christ saved me and my whole family. Praise God! I encourage you to put your trust in Jesus Christ, for He is the one true God.

 **Govind Sathiya Seelan** is the founder of Alleluia Full Gospel Ministries (Mission India), a religious and charitable nonprofit in India. His work over many years of ministry has included distributing food and clothing to the poor and needy, providing vocational training to widows and children of martyrs, planting churches, and founding a Bible college. He has established more than one thousand churches and baptized in excess of a half-million converts. Today, traveling between India and the United States, he continues his missionary efforts. For more information, write govindsathiyaseelan@gmail.com or visit www.shekinahglobalmedia.net.

13

Jesus, the Missionary, and the Tsunami

When the enemy comes in like a
flood, the Spirit of the LORD will
lift up a standard against him.

ISAIAH 59:19

*M*Y NAME IS Dayalan Sanders. I was born into a Christian family in Sri Lanka in 1954. Growing up, I wasn't religious, but from reading the Scriptures I eventually developed a burning desire to be close to God. In the mid-1970s I committed my life to Jesus, determining to follow Him 100 percent.

In the 1980s I immigrated to America, obtained my citizenship, and did relief work in Sri Lanka, where there was great need resulting from the civil war. I felt God calling me to minister to the orphans, who were like sheep without a shepherd. In 1994 I sold my townhouse and belongings and returned to Sri Lanka. I built The Samaritan Children's Home in a village called Navalady that occupies a narrow peninsula on Sri Lanka's east coast.

In 2004 I experienced a series of miracles and divine interventions.

On Christmas Eve 2004 we invited the village to our annual children's day program, which included a nativity, plays, and songs. In everything we tried to present the gospel of the Lord Jesus Christ. Many villagers came, 90 percent of whom were Hindus and Muslims.

On Christmas Day we again invited the village for our Christmas service, and many people came. When everyone left, I was exhausted. I went to bed around 5:30 p.m. Usually before I turn in, I check our complex to make sure the gates are locked, the lights are on, and our watchmen are in place. I also make sure the outboard motor is removed from our boat to prevent it from being stolen. That day I was so tired that I didn't check it; the motor stayed on the boat.

On Sunday, December 26, I awakened to the sound of footsteps; someone was running down the corridor. My wife, Kohila, burst through the bedroom door with an expression of absolute horror on her face.

"The sea...is...coming!" she stammered.

I thought it was just a big wave that crashed against the shore and rolled over into our yard. I said, "Calm down. God is with us. Go and gather the children; bring them here." So I sent her.

I walked onto the veranda and looked toward the sea. I couldn't believe what I saw. On the horizon was an enormous wall of sea stretching from one end of the beach to the other. It wasn't a wave. It was an ocean riding on top of another ocean—caused by the undersea earthquake in the Indian Ocean. The tsunami created by the earthquake on Christmas Eve ultimately killed more than two hundred thousand people in fourteen countries.

There was a thunderous roar, like a thousand charging freight trains. It was coming at us with such speed. I knew instantly there would be no safe place on the ground.

"Everybody—get to the boat!" I yelled.

I ran toward our boat, which was docked at the lagoon. By then many of the children had run outside. I shouted, urging them toward the boat. They came rushing. We had ten seconds to board the boat. As I mentioned, I had left the motor hooked to the boat the night before. It was still attached, which is a miracle in itself.

Desperate by now, I asked if anyone had seen my daughter. A moment later one of the older girls thrust my toddler into my arms. I heaved her into the boat, along with the other small children, as the older ones and my orphanage staff climbed aboard.

The sea had already breached our complex. It had demolished part of it, and our vehicles were being swept into the lagoon. Then Isaiah 59:19 came to my mind. I got the courage, faced the wave, and quoted as loud as I could, "'When the enemy comes in like a flood, the Spirit of the Lord will lift up a standard against him!' On the strength of the Scriptures, I command you in the name of Jesus Christ to stop!"

What happened next was a miracle. I thought I was imagining it at the time. That massive wall of water that was seconds away from engulfing us became sluggish, like it was straining against an invisible wall. It was as if some invisible force was holding it back. It was trying to break free, but something was restraining it. The only force that could've stopped it was the power of God. And God, with His powerful hand, held the wave for us, and gave us time to escape.

Everyone was petrified. I shouted at the boatman to start the motor. He yanked the starter cord, and the engine sputtered instantly to life—something that had *never* happened before. Usually you have to pull that cord about five times before the motor starts. That was another miracle.

As we took off into the lagoon in our dangerously overloaded boat, crammed with more than twenty people, that wall of water overwhelmed the orphanage, rushing in with a thunderous roar, demolishing everything in its path.

I looked and, to my horror, my wife, Kohila, was on the pier! In all the chaos, she hadn't been able to make it to the boat in time. Suddenly a wave hit her from behind, throwing her into the water. Miraculously she landed near our boat. We frantically pulled her aboard, then headed into the lagoon.

As we made for the lagoon's mouth, our boat was broadsided and nearly capsized by the torrent pouring over the peninsula. The children were terrified. We were praying, "God, help us!"

About forty people were clinging to a massive banyan tree on the shore when three huge waves hit it. The third wave ripped the tree off its roots and all those people drowned in front of us. If it had such power to uproot a huge tree and toss it like a matchstick, then the fact that our eighteen-foot fiberglass boat was surviving the tsunami was God's mercy.

We stayed atop that body of water for about ninety minutes, battling the waves.

Eventually we made it to the city of Batticaloa, about two kilometers away on the opposite shore. We had survived the deadly tsunami. I dropped our children and staff at another church, then went back, picking up survivors. Later I met some villagers who'd climbed on top of trees and survived the onslaught.

"We didn't stand a chance," they said, "because when the sea crashed into the village it came with such speed and fury it wiped us out. But when it got on your land, it slowed down, and that gave you a chance. What made it slow down? Was it the density of the trees or buildings?"

"There's nothing on earth that could've held it back but the power of God," I said. "I called upon God and commanded it in the name of Jesus, who two thousand years ago commanded the waves and they obeyed [see Mark 4:39]. God did the same for us and gave us those precious few seconds we needed to escape."

We were eye to eye with the tsunami and should have been swept away. And we would have been, had it not been for God's merciful divine intervention.

Dayalan Sanders is a pastor and the founder and director of Samaritan Children's Home in Mylampavelly, Sri Lanka, where his ministry work includes caring for orphans, teaching, and preaching the gospel. For more information, write dayalansanders@yahoo.com or visit www.samaritanchildrenshome.org.

14

The Thanksgiving Miracle

But He [Jesus] was wounded for our
transgressions, He was bruised for our
iniquities; the chastisement for our peace was
upon Him, and by His stripes we are healed.

ISAIAH 53:5

*M*Y NAME IS Billy Lamont. I'm a poet and a follower of Jesus Christ. I was born in 1962 and grew up in North Babylon, New York. I'd like to share a story of a very personal divine intervention in my life. I hope it enriches your life. I believe it has underlying truths that can be applied to us all.

In 1989 I became very sick on Thanksgiving Day. I kept getting nauseous and vomiting. It eventually became dry heaves, and I couldn't get any relief from the pain. I went to St. John's Hospital in Smithtown, New York. When I arrived, the staff had fun with me a bit because it was Thanksgiving. They were teasing me, saying things like, "Oh, did you eat too much turkey?" or, "Poor dear! You got a bellyache?"

I kept saying, "No, really, I'm not one to complain. Something is wrong with me." They did some tests, and after many hours they determined I needed to be admitted because the level of one of my pancreatic fluids was too high. It was serious.

A few hours later some doctors told me, "The level being too high in your pancreas indicates that you either have cancer, a serious liver problem, or, best-case scenario, an ulcer."

I remember thinking, "Wow. I can't believe this." I was surprised because I'd always been healthy, and I didn't have anything with which to compare this experience. I was sad and afraid, as it didn't seem like

56

there were any good options. For support I shared this news with my family and friends (who all were very concerned), and I began praying.

In the days that followed I was given many different tests. I was put into a room with pregnant women and given a sonogram, which was a humbling experience. I joked with the women in the waiting area, saying, "If I'm pregnant, I don't know who the father is!" to help relieve some of my worry. Thankfully, the sonogram came back negative—my organs looked OK.

The next day I was to be given another test in which they would knock me out and put a scope down my throat to check my stomach for ulcers and other things. At that time my mom belonged to a prayer chain at Faith Tabernacle Church in West Babylon, New York. The prayer chain worked like this: if someone had a prayer request he or she would call a person on the list and the two people would pray together; then that person would call the next person on the list and those two people would pray, and so on. So my mom called her friend to pray with her for me.

Before she could say why she was calling, my mom's friend interrupted and said, "You know, it was really weird…I prayed last night, and when I went to sleep I had a dream of a young man in the hospital having a medical device put down his throat into his stomach as a test. I felt the Lord Jesus say to me, 'He's OK, and there's nothing to worry about. I am there with him.'"

My mom exclaimed, "That's my son! He's having that test tomorrow! I can't believe you just said that! I was calling to tell you my son is in that situation!" So they prayed together and thanked the Lord Jesus.

When my mom shared this story with me, it brought me a lot of peace. It had extra significance for me because of the way I'd originally become a Christian six years earlier.

In 1983 I was searching for the truth about God, and my friend recommended that I pray to Jesus. So that's what I did—I prayed to Jesus while I was alone in my bedroom. I said, "Jesus, if You're real please show Yourself to me and I'll believe in You—but You have to reveal Yourself to me."

Amazingly, Jesus answered that prayer instantly, powerfully, and beautifully. I had a vision of Jesus and felt the electricity of the Holy Spirit while I was praying. Again, not in any church, but alone in my bedroom. It was a very deep, personal experience. Since that time I've been a whole-hearted believer and follower of Christ.

So, six years later, in my hour of need, for Jesus to speak to my mom's friend through a dream and for me to receive that message meant a great deal to me. My fears started to go; I could feel my faith increasing.

What's amazing is that they gave me test after test at the hospital, and they started eliminating different things. They couldn't find any cancer, couldn't find any liver problem, and couldn't find an ulcer—everything came back negative!

Eventually the doctor said to me: "Quite frankly, we're perplexed about the whole situation. We don't know why you had such a high level of this pancreatic fluid. We're surprised because usually in cases like this it's very serious. But the levels in your pancreas have stabilized, and we have no explanation for this. We're going to call it 'pancreatitis with a question mark.'"

They then discharged me, and I was fine. I knew in my heart the Lord Jesus had healed me.

Reflecting back, I remember that about a month before I'd gotten sick, I'd prayed to God for more empathy. I'd been reading in the Bible about how Jesus said to visit the sick, feed the poor, and visit people in prison. (See Matthew 25:35–46.) I remember particularly praying about visiting people in hospitals. Was I really having empathy for others? I always tried to, as I wanted to be a genuine Christian, but I had a hard time empathizing with people who were ill. I had no experience with it myself, so how genuine could I be? I was digging for something deeper when I prayed that prayer.

Even though it was scary going through that experience, I believe it was a gift to me—an answered prayer; it gave me more compassion and empathy for other people. Now I know how it feels to be helpless and in the hospital. I also know that through my relationship with Jesus, I was healed. The same Jesus who lived two thousand years ago is still healing people today. It's my prayer today that, whatever you're going through, you'll pray to Jesus and that He will touch and heal you too.

Billy Lamont is an American poet who takes an avant-garde approach to writing, music, politics, and performance art. At the heart of his poetry is the passion to inspire hope and be a voice for everyday people. His unique vision for poetry in the twenty-first century, combined with his belief in the power of words for creation, reformation, and healing, has brought him international recognition. His poems encourage dignity and life and have been a catalyst for many people to live in a more loving way. They have been the inspiration for some readers to help for the first time with personal and social reform. Billy lives on Long Island, New York. For more information, write TOPm777@gmail.com or visit www.billylamont.com or www.twitter.com/poetbillylamont.

15

Coming to America

Forget the former things; do not dwell on
the past. See, I am doing a new thing!
ISAIAH 43:18–19, NIV

M<small>Y NAME IS</small> Anupam Bhomia. I was born in 1974 in Jaipur,
India. God brought me through many trials, performed miracles, and
enabled me to realize my dream of coming to America.

I was raised Hindu, but one day when I was still young, a very dedicated Christian woman invited my mother to a healing crusade being
held by a visiting American pastor. At the meeting the pastor called my
mother out of the crowd. Although they'd never met, he knew what was
happening in her life. She received a prophetic word and personal prayer,
and she was deeply moved. She returned the second and third nights of
the crusade and knew within three days she'd found the true God in
Jesus Christ.

I was young, and my mother didn't tell me much about Jesus. In fact,
she didn't know much about Jesus herself, but we knew if we prayed to
Him, things would happen. We didn't even know how to pray, but we'd
read from a Christian songbook we had. My mother would say, "Jesus,
help us." As soon as we would pray, God would answer.

We started attending the church that our friend attended. Because we
were from a Hindu background, visiting a Christian church was considered shameful. We'd hide the fact that we were going. The church was
in a westerly direction, but to prevent people from discovering where
we were going, we'd board the eastbound bus, then change buses several
times before boarding the westbound bus to take us to church.

My mother covered her face and put a hat on me. The parishioners were so loving and prayed for us individually. Going to church gave us new strength and hope. Things were slowly starting to happen. It took years, but God gave us peace and strength—strength to live and to face our Hindu relatives.

I was eight when I gave my life to Jesus, and I have been so privileged to know Him since then.

Walk of Faith

Because my mother became a Christian through an American missionary, I fell in love with America. People said, "You'll go to America, earn dollars, and become rich." I had a different love for America. I believed America was the lighthouse of Christianity—and it is. In northern India you don't see many foreign Christians; but if you look, the most courageous, hard-working people are Americans. America gives so much to needy countries. It's great to see. So I loved America. I was about twelve when I sent my first letter to the American embassy, requesting information on how to go to America. They sent me a brochure.

Growing up, I saved every cent my mother gave me. I would write to American colleges, but writing letters doesn't get you to America. You need about $80,000. When you apply for a student visa, the consular officer needs to see how you'll support yourself for four years while you're there. They ask questions such as: "What's the purpose of studying in America when the same course is available in India? How will you support yourself?"

I didn't have any funds because Indian money converts to very little in US dollars. They wouldn't give a visa to a young, unmarried person with no family ties because they know he isn't returning. He's going to live there; maybe become an illegal immigrant or pay an American to marry him so he can get a green card. That's what many people do.

I didn't know all that then. I just wanted to go to America. In twelfth grade everyone was preparing for the medical or engineering college-entrance exams. I was preparing for the SATs.

People said, "He's nuts."

A close relative once asked, "What are you doing with your career? A friend's son got into medical college. Another's son became a doctor. His brother became an engineer."

I thought, "I just hope I get through my SATs."

The Bible says to have faith. It says, "Faith is the substance of things hoped for, the evidence of things not seen" (Heb. 11:1). I was walking by faith. I prayed, "Jesus, I'm asking You the most impossible thing. I don't know how You'll do it, but I know You will."

When I was nineteen, I had about eight friends who all got into medical or engineering schools. I was doing nothing. I had only a high school diploma.

I knew my father was angry. He's a doctor, and he wanted me to be a doctor. Education is huge in India. It's like you must be a doctor or engineer or you cannot survive in the country. I knew that if I didn't get a medical or engineering degree, I might be thrown out of the house.

My mother would say, "Anupam, just pray." Later she said, "If going to America isn't working out, why don't you go get a liberal arts degree, at least?"

I said, "No, Mom. If I give up and do something else, that means I don't have faith." It was easy to say that, but each day was a battle. I'd wake up every day and see the anger on my father's face. Even at that age, it was so stressful that I had chest pains. I wondered, "How will I survive in this house?"

My mother and I started praying fervently in the mornings from four o'clock until seven o'clock. I was nineteen, with no hope or career. Nothing happened immediately, but I had more faith and knew something definitely would happen. My love for America remained strong.

In 1995 an Indian pastor had a healing crusade. My mother went to him, saying, "I know you pray and things happen. Please pray for my son. His only desire is to go to America."

He said, "Sister, I cannot help you much with this, but there's a Bible college in Texas. Write to them. Maybe they can help you."

I wrote to the Bible college, Christ for the Nations Institute in Dallas. They asked me to submit an application. The Holy Spirit told me to write my testimony and send it with the application, which I did. I heard back from them, and was shocked as they granted me a tuition scholarship of $5,000!

I told a relative, "They'll give me $5,000. Would you be kind enough to give me another $5,000 for room and board?"

He said, "If you return with a Bible college diploma, that money is wasted. It's my life savings." Back then, $5,000 was about four years' salary for this relative. He saved all that money. Why would he give it to me to go to Bible school in America? I could've gone to any Bible college in India.

"Holy Spirit, please make a way," I prayed. "I know You don't want to disappoint us. I'm Yours. I'm not Hindu, and all these people are watching me."

My relative finally agreed, saying, "I can arrange $5,000." My next challenge was getting a visa, which was nearly impossible. The Bible school program was for two years. The US embassy wanted me to show that I had $22,000, plus round-trip airfare. I only had $5,000, and I didn't even really *have* the $5,000 because my relative was still arranging the money.

Passing the Test

I went to the American embassy for my visa interview, and there were more than two hundred people in line. There were six windows, and at each window people were being denied their visas, one after the next. The line moved slowly, and the closer I got to the window, the harder my heart beat. I was so nervous I could actually hear it beating.

I prayed, "Lord, You must speak to me." I took out my Bible, and it opened to Isaiah 43:18: "Forget the former things; do not dwell on the past. See, I am doing a new thing! Now it springs up; do you not perceive it? I am making a way in the wilderness and streams in the wasteland" (NIV).

"What good words!" I thought, but I wasn't convinced. I closed my Bible. After several minutes, I said, "Lord, I want to talk to You, please." I reopened my Bible, and it opened to the same page in Isaiah. I was thinking, "This page must be sticky. There must be something wrong here." So I flipped through all the pages, like you would when shuffling a deck of cards. I closed my Bible and opened it again. The same page, with the same scripture, came up again! I was in deep anxiety at this point and asked the Lord again to speak to me. There was a south Indian woman standing behind me.

Suddenly, she shook my shoulder and said, "You'll get a visa, brother. Don't worry. The Lord just told me." Can you believe that out of the two hundred people, the woman behind me was a prophet, and a Spirit-filled, born-again Christian? She got a message from the Holy Spirit telling her I'd get a visa! I said I believed her to show how strong my faith was, but, truthfully, my faith was shaky. People around me had suits, ties, and shiny shoes, and every day there were hundreds of people lined up. This was only one embassy in one city. Given the chance, I think everyone in India would come to America in a minute! Very few actually get visas.

I was wearing khaki pants, my shoelace was untied, and I thought, "I'm presenting myself badly, and I'm here for an interview." But I said, "Lord, if You're with me, who can be against me?" I prayed, "I cover these counters with the blood of Jesus."

My turn came—window six. The embassy woman said, "Come here." Then she said, "Stop." I didn't understand that she was actually calling another guy up to give her paperwork as I approached. She said to me, "Stay there, sir. You look like you're in too much of a hurry to go to America." I thought I had blown it.

I went back to the line, thinking, "That's it. I lost it." Then I was called to window four. At the counter was a young woman, no more than thirty years old.

She asked for my paperwork, and I gave her my passport and Bible college admission letter. She said, "All right, name the Gospels."

"Matthew, Mark, Luke, John," I answered.

"OK, tell me what happened to Saul on the way."

I was thinking, "Saul...who is Saul?" I was so nervous I forgot who Saul was.

Again she said, "What happened to Saul on the way?"

Finally it came to me and I answered, "He heard the voice from heaven say, 'Saul, Saul, why do you persecute Me?'"

"Great," she said. "Then what happened?"

"Then he became a disciple of Christ, and most of the New Testament was written by Saul."

She said, "All right. You'll get your visa." She stamped it, "Approved." That was it. No financial records, no questions about why I was going—nothing. She gave me a receipt and said, "Go over there and pay the deposit fee." I went with shaking hands to pay the fee, and after I recovered from the shock and disbelief at what had just happened, I returned to the counter to thank her. She wasn't there—she was gone. God sends angels at certain times and places in our lives. I believe this was one of those times.

I came to America and attended the Bible college in Texas. After graduating, I moved to New York City, and it wasn't easy. I didn't know anyone at first. I lived in the streets and subways, and even went without food for as long as twelve days. Some Hindus I shared a room with for a while threw me out because I was a Christian convert, but God never left me. By His grace I made it to America through a series of miracles and divine interventions.

Eventually I acclimated to life here. I'm so blessed. Jesus has never let me down.

Anupam Bhomia works today full time in New York City. He and his wife live with their two children on Long Island. For more information, write anupam.bhomia@gmail.com.

16

Blessed With Cancer

And we know that all things work together
for good to those who love God, to those who
are the called according to His purpose.

ROMANS 8:28

$\mathcal{M}$Y NAME IS Daniel Fazzina, and God has intervened in my life many times. One of those times was when I was in the midst of a health crisis.

I felt the dull ache of death in my chest—the throbbing, the *pounding*! I just wanted it to stop—*please*! I saw dim fluorescent lights and heard distant, frantic, unfamiliar voices. I was on my back, moving down a long hallway. But where was I? A wave of nausea churned in my gut. I cringed, and vomit exploded from my mouth.

I felt something bite me. "What was that?" I wondered. "Get it off of me!" I felt the cold sting of thin steel pierce my flesh, and a burning sensation climbed from the wound up into the veins of my arm. Faces flashed into my view like ghosts, vanishing before my confused mind could recognize them, teasing me, taunting me.

I glimpsed a middle-aged man with a furrowed brow peering closely into my face. Why was he touching my eyelids? There were bright lights, flashes of white, then a young black woman with a kind, nervous face hovering over me. Was she an angel? It seemed as if my eyes were rolling around in their sockets like loose marbles while a spectral blacksmith used my head as an anvil, pounding me relentlessly with his invisible hammer. I heard my name through the clamor like a distant echo: "Daniel? Daniel! He's going out! Doctor!"

Another flash, this time something vaguely familiar, deep brown eyes.

Those eyes—could it be Mom? Yes! I wanted to cry out but my voice refused to comply. My tongue was tied in a knot, and the room was spinning, but Mother was there. A look of sadness mixed with terror covered her face. Her loving eyes had ballooned to twice their normal size. I focused on them, somewhat comforted knowing she was there as consciousness fled from me.

Little did I know, this initial emergency room visit would be the beginning of my family's descent into the valley of the shadow of death. It was the summer of 2002, and I was twenty-seven years old. The doctors found a massive, cancerous tumor inside my chest. The diagnosis was lymphoma. The tumor was positioned just above my heart, and it was larger than my heart. As it grew, it began crushing my pulmonary artery, starving me of oxygen and literally suffocating me.

The oncologists said it was inoperable, and that they would try to treat it with medication, but they weren't sure if it would respond. If it didn't, they assured me I'd be dead within months—three at the most.

What do you do when you hear news like that? It's impossible to know what the "right" response should be. I felt a mixture of disbelief, shock, and numbness.

The following months were the most challenging and glorious of my life, filled with doctors' visits, prayer meetings, pain, prophecies, medical tests, visions, love, and support. As a follower of Jesus since my childhood, I knew I was God's child and that He could heal me if He wanted to. It was in this season of my life that God taught me to completely depend on Him. I remember being alone one night in my hospital bed, literally suffocating. I looked up to the ceiling and offered up a simple prayer. "Lord," I said, "I know I'm Your child. If You want to take me, I'll go with You." The Bible says that for the believer, to be absent from the body is to be present with the Lord (2 Cor. 5:8), and I believe that. I continued, "But if You want to heal me and let me live, I will do my best to continue to serve You, and to share with the world Your goodness, love, mercy, and power." I was a broken man, totally thrown onto the mercy of God, praying like Jesus did, "Not my will, but Yours, be done" (Luke 22:42).

In late December I went in for my follow-up PET scan. It had been three months since I started chemotherapy, and this was the halfway-point scan to gauge the progress. The doctors were hoping (and my loved ones were praying) the tumor would be smaller and that the treatment was working. Well, God really answered everyone's prayers because when I got the results, the tumor was not just smaller, it was completely *gone*! When I saw the pictures with no sign of the tumor that had so ominously threatened my life only months before, I looked up to heaven and with tears in my eyes thanked Jesus for His goodness and mercy.

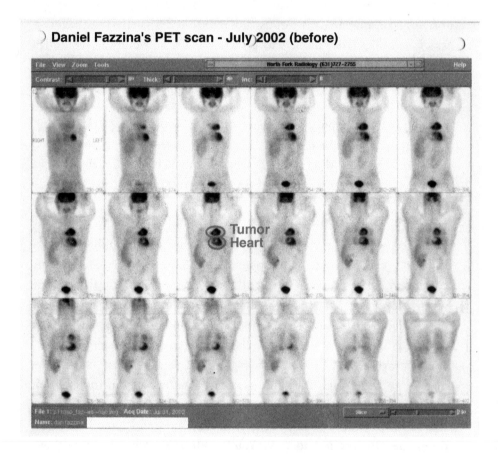

Daniel Fazzina's PET scan - July 2002 (before)

Daniel Fazzina's PET scan - December 2002 (after)

Ironic as it may sound, God used a terrible, deadly disease to bless me abundantly. All the grace and blessings that resulted from my being sick could fill its own book, but here are a few examples:

- My faith in Jesus and the knowledge that He is in control of my life, no matter how bad things look, was made more real to me through my experience. "Head knowledge" was tested and turned into "experiential knowledge."

- The faith of many people around me was strengthened after having witnessed the miracles that occurred during the crisis.

- Many relationships with friends and family were strengthened.

- My relationship with my girlfriend, Sahani, was strengthened. We were drawn closer together in prayer, and it helped to mature us in our relationship with each other and with God. Today we are happily married and so blessed!

I have been honored to share my testimony at many churches, on radio shows, even on Fox News and television programs such as *The 700 Club* and TBN's *Praise the Lord*. I now host my own radio show called *Divine Intervention*, on which I interview others who have experienced miracles. This led to the publication of this book.

Many other blessings came out of my being ill, but it's enough to say that the same Jesus who walked the earth two thousand years ago performing miracles and healing people is still alive today and still doing miracles. He is real and He wants a relationship with you. I pray that you don't take my word for it, however. I pray you will take a chance on Jesus, that you will give Him an opportunity to show you, and that you will experience Him for yourself. He loves you so much.

Daniel Fazzina, a native New Yorker, is the host of the *Divine Intervention Radio Show*, which can be heard on radio stations across the country and at www.divineinterventionradio.com. He resides in Virginia with his magnificent bride, Sahani, and their lovable Cavalier King Charles spaniel/papillon/Jack Russell terrier, Pumpkin. Connect with Daniel on Twitter: @DanielFazzina1 or www.facebook.com/divineinterventionradio.

17

Fruit for God

I am the vine, you are the branches. He who
abides in Me, and I in him, bears much fruit.

JOHN 15:5

MY NAME IS Joe Paskewich. I was born in 1955 in New
London, Connecticut, where I've lived most of my life. I'm a pastor and
radio station manager. God has performed many divine interventions to
get me where I am today.

Although I grew up in a wonderful family, I dropped out of school
after eighth grade and started hanging around some rough people. Since
I had little supervision, I quickly got into some bad things, including
drugs and alcohol. It was downhill from there. I was a disappointment
to my parents. I was constantly in trouble with the law, getting arrested
often. Life was a total downward spiral until I moved out at age fifteen.

There were times in my life when I wanted to connect with Jesus, but
I really didn't know who He was or what it meant to know Him. I came
to faith in Jesus when I was twenty, but from ages fifteen to twenty, I was
involved in all kinds of crazy, illegal activities.

When I was about nineteen, I had everything I thought would make a
person happy, and I hadn't worked much for any of it; any job I would get
I'd always lose. But I was in what I thought were ideal conditions. I was
living in a cabin in the woods. I had some dogs, some drugs, and lots of
good music—but I was totally empty.

It was then that I met the first real Christian I ever recall interacting
with: the sister of the girl I was living with. She came over one day to tell
me about Jesus and what happened to her. At that time I was looking
for something. I'd been reading Eastern literature. This girl told me I

71

needed to be born again. Since I'd been reading about reincarnation and wasn't familiar with biblical language or the concept of being spiritually born again as Jesus said, I thought she was telling me I needed to be reincarnated.

"If anybody needs to be born again, it's you," she said. I agreed—if anybody needed to be born again, it was me.

Then she said, "You can do it right now."

I thought she was telling me to kill myself. That's the only thing that made sense to me—that if I killed myself, then I'd be born again and come back in another state. I told her I wasn't ready. She continued trying to convince me that the best thing I could do was to do it right then. I was totally perplexed. I told her, "Maybe some other time." Then she invited me to church. I said I'd go with her, but I never did.

I found out later that she saw how desperate I was and began gathering weekly with some friends for what they called "the Joe Paskewich prayer meeting." They prayed for me every week. Within about a year after that encounter with her I came to know Christ.

Hitchhiking to Find God

Several divine interventions led to my coming to faith in Christ. At that point I had some friends in Arizona. Many people from our area in Connecticut were moving to Arizona. Being close to the Mexican border, there were plenty of opportunities to get marijuana, so my friends and I moved to Arizona.

When I arrived, I discovered I was even emptier than when I left. I attribute that to the prayer meeting being held for me. My mind was constantly turning toward God, and I was becoming very aware of how empty I was.

Across the street from the house where we lived was a park. One day I was there swinging on the swings in the middle of the day (I didn't do anything; I hadn't had a job in years). The girl I was living with was with me. Suddenly I burst out into tears, and she asked, "What's wrong?"

"I'm going to hell," I said. "I don't even know what hell is, but I'm definitely going."

"If you're going to hell," she said, "you're going without me."

And that was the end of that relationship. She packed up and left. I think she thought I was cracking up—and I think I was. I was extremely desperate. We split up, and I was in despair. I didn't know what to do with my life, so I did the only thing I knew to do—I found the number for a monastery, called them, and said I wanted to join. They asked me some questions, then told me I'd have to get some training and education. I wasn't prepared for that. My attempt to get into the monastery to connect with God failed.

So I just started walking. I walked away from the house and everything else and began a homeless jaunt around the United States. I guess I was looking for God, and I'm convinced He was looking for me too. By that point I think we were ready to connect. It was soon after this that I had another amazing, wild, divine intervention.

I was hitchhiking around the country, taking rides to wherever people were going. I'd stay there for a while, then get out and hitchhike some more. This was 1975, when hitchhiking was common. In October 1975 I was in Kansas City in morning commuter traffic. Nobody picks you up in commuter traffic—it's too dangerous to pull over. I was walking down a four-lane highway with my back to the traffic and my thumb out.

As I was hitchhiking, there was a van in the far left lane. I saw this van pull into the next lane and almost cause an accident. Then it pulled into the next lane to the right. Kansas City is pretty flat and the roads go for quite a while, so you can see far, and the traffic was moving fast. As the van rapidly pulled over from lane to lane to lane, it caught my attention. Finally it got to the shoulder of the road. A door opened and a guy jumped out. He had long hair that flopped up and down, and he signaled me to come, like has was offering me a ride.

I thought, "I don't even know where I'm going—and I'm pretty nuts—but that guy is crazier than me! I'm not going with him! If he wants me to go with him, he's going to have to wait for me to walk up there. I'm going to hitchhike in the meantime, and if I get a ride, I'm taking it."

I got to the van, and he asked me where I was going. I gave my typical response: "Where are you going?"

"Connecticut," he said.

"I'm going to Connecticut too," I said.

Three people were inside the van: a guy driving, a girl in the front passenger seat, and the guy with the floppy hair, who was sitting in the back.

"This is crazy," I thought. "I shouldn't have gotten into the van with these people." The girl in the front was looking at me and smiling with a big grin. She would turn around, look at me and grin, then turn back to the front; then she'd turn around again and look at me and grin. I thought it was very strange. I'd gotten many rides with different people, but this was the strangest yet.

Then she said, "God told us to pick you up."

"*What?*" I exclaimed. I had heard stories about people who talked to God—now I was in a van with some. I wondered what was going to happen to me. I'd never experienced anything like these people. I honestly thought they were going to kill me. Those were the days of the Manson Family, and all kinds of crazy stuff was happening. I thought we'd end up on some farm somewhere, and it would be the end for me. I was trying to figure out a way to escape from the van.

As we were riding along, the guy in the back said the strangest thing to me. He had a guitar, and he asked, "Do you want me to sing you a song?" I thought the people were crazy, so I didn't want to say no to him.

"Yeah, sure," I said. "Sing a song."

He started singing, and one of the lines was, "Accept Him with your whole heart, and with your own two hands; with one hand reach out to Jesus and with the other, bring a friend."

I thought, "Man, that's it! That's what I need to do!"

I think it may have been that moment when I really opened my heart to Jesus. Those simple words resonated so deep within me. Later he asked if I wanted him to read the Bible to me, and I said sure. He read from Proverbs, and I thought, "Whoever wrote that book knows what they're talking about." It was as if I were hearing about my life and my lack of knowing how to live properly. Within about an hour of being in the van, I wanted to be close to Jesus and know more about the Bible.

I learned that the guy in the back had written a book with a publishing house in New Jersey called Logos. It was a huge company that published many books during the charismatic renewal of the 1970s. He'd written a book on the subject of giving, and he was going to New Jersey to see his publisher. The girl in the passenger seat was going to Connecticut. She'd moved to California, become a Christian, and was returning to Connecticut to tell her family about Jesus. The other guy was driving everybody.

I was becoming attracted to whatever it was they had, and I noticed something else that fascinated me. Here were these two guys and this one girl in the van, and they treated this girl with absolute purity, as though she were their sister. That spoke deeply to me because most of my friends at that time didn't show the same respect toward women. I was fascinated by how they treated, respected, and protected her. It wasn't just the words, the Bible, and the songs, but I saw something in the way they lived. In 1975 everybody was talking about love, and they truly loved one another and were very open with their lives with me. I was really starting to see some love.

As we drove along, although I wanted to be with them, I felt like I needed to get away. Something was telling me that I needed to get out at some juncture. It was two o'clock in the morning when they dropped me off outside of Chicago.

Coming Home

When they left, I prayed, "Jesus, I want what they have. I don't know everything that it is, but I know it's You. I want You in my life." At that moment, Jesus came into my life and I honestly felt different. I know that not everyone feels different when they accept Christ, but I just felt "different." I knew that Jesus was the One I wanted. I had no Bible—all the Bible I knew was what the guy had read to me from Proverbs and one chapter of Jeremiah.

Within several weeks I was back in Connecticut, wanting to tell my friends about Christ, and I had another cool experience. The only other Christian I knew was the girl who'd told me I needed to be born again. I called her, and she took me to an unusual church filled with all young people. All the pastor did was sit on a stool, play a guitar, read from the Bible, and then ask people if they wanted to be born again. People always responded. Sometimes they'd pray for people's needs if people were sick, and it seemed like God answered those prayers.

One day the pastor was teaching and said, "If you're born again, lift your hand for a minute." So I raised my hand. Then I heard someone say, "Hey, Joe!" I turned and looked—it was the people from the van! The guy had his thumb up like, yes!

When the meeting was over, he came over and said, "Man! It's good to see some fruit!"

I didn't know anything about the Christian life, vernacular or vocabulary, so I was thinking, "Fruit? What do you mean, 'fruit'?" I later discovered what he meant, but I was clueless then. He wasn't insulting me. He meant that the simple sharing of the gospel, and the sharing of one's life, was causing people to turn to Jesus. It was producing fruit in the sense that my turning to Christ was "fruit" from his testimony.

It was miraculous for those people to be there and for me to meet them again. I reflect on this experience often because it was the power of God's Word and the power of the love those people showed me.

Years later I started a church in Connecticut where my friends were. One of the guys who taught me to play the guitar when I was a teenager is one of our key worship leaders. Some of our key ushers are the people I used to get into trouble with. It's interesting to see what God has done in the lives of all these people.

The girl from the van came to the church several times over the years when she was in the area visiting family. The first time I saw her sitting in church I was so happy to see her, so I told the congregation the whole hitchhiking story about the crazy guy pulling across multiple lanes on the highway. Afterward she came to me and said, "Joe, I have to tell you, that's not really the way the story goes."

I thought, "It had better go that way because I've been telling it that way everywhere!"

"Here's what happened," she said. "We were driving through the city and there was all this traffic and when Gary [the driver] saw you, he said God told him to give you a ride. He decided to pull off at the next exit and circle back around and pick you up because he couldn't pull over."

"After he pulled off, exited, and re-entered the highway, we got caught in the traffic and couldn't find you. Gary was driving all over town looking for you, and then we started discouraging him. We said, 'Gary, the guy's not here. We looked for him. We're doing our best, trying to obey God, but the guy's gone.' Gary said, 'He's got to be here, because God told me to pick him up.'"

"When he finally saw you again, he went absolutely ballistic, like everything in him told him he had to do whatever it took to get over there and pick you up."

That explained all the erratic driving and craziness. When I think about this, I think how desperate God is out there looking for us. He's looking for people. There was somebody on my end praying for me every week, and I started getting miserable and empty and started looking for God. At the same time He had other people in another place He was speaking to, telling them to pick me up. They were just the right people for the right time. It was an unbelievable, fascinating, divine encounter—by appointment. It was a miracle how God spoke to different people at different times in different ways and brought everything together.

Now when I tell the story, I tell everybody afterward that the story didn't go exactly that way, and then I tell the rest of it. God was desperately looking for me and using this person who was obedient to pick me up. It's so cool the way God puts everybody together. Now I understand why the girl was grinning at me in the van when they picked me up. They'd finally found me, and that was joyful for them. They were probably thinking, "What's God doing here? What's He up to?" They knew something supernatural was happening.

That's my story of how God got hold of my life. He used that sequence of events to draw me to Himself, and eventually I came back into town and wanted to tell my friends about Jesus. I founded a church, where I still am today.

Jesus changed my life, and I pray that you put your trust in Jesus, and that He changes your life too.

Joe Paskewich describes himself as "one grateful human being trying to make a difference." He is the founder and lead pastor of Calvary Chapel Eastern Connecticut, a multisite, multicultural, intergenerational group of believers gathering in Jesus's name. He and his wife live in New London, Connecticut, and have one son. For more information, write paskewich@gmail.com or visit www.paskewich.com or www.revelation320.org.

18

An Islamic Warrior Finds Peace in Christ

Come to Me, all you who labor and are
heavy laden, and I will give you rest.

MATTHEW 11:28

MY NAME IS Zachariah Anani. I was born in Beirut, Lebanon, in 1958. I come from a line of Muslim clergy. My great-grandfather and grandfather were both imams. My father was an alcoholic and a womanizer, which prevented him from becoming an imam. My family had high hopes for me and wanted me to continue the Anani line of clergy. At age three I started religious training at an Islamic school. By age thirteen I could recite the prayers and had some of the Quran memorized.

God blessed me with a strong body. At thirteen I was bigger than most kids my age, and by sixteen I was one hundred eighty pounds of pure muscle. I was very rebellious and didn't want to be in school. At that time (the early seventies), the Palestinians were marching through our streets. They amazed me with their weaponry and machinery. I wanted to be that holy warrior who would knock on heaven's doors with my enemies' skulls, throw them at Allah's feet, and say, "Here's my gift to you. Now let me enter your heaven." That is Islamic theology. Islam is the religion of the book and the sword. You're a warrior and a man from age thirteen. You're trained to be either a warrior or a religious teacher.

The Palestinians had come to Lebanon to occupy their own land like they did in Jordan. But the Lebanese army hit them hard and pushed them back. So they began forming small fragments—some political, some religious. Islam is both religious and political.

Since I wanted to be like those warriors and serve my Allah like

79

them, I joined one of those offshoot groups. I was actually fighting other Muslims, although politically and psychologically I was trained to wage holy war against the Jews. Early on you're trained to hate and kill Jews and, if necessary, Christians and Americans.

I understood all this in training, and my family approved. They were happy because in Islamic doctrine, only the warrior who dies in battle killing his enemies will reach heaven, and his family will be feared and respected. That's how I came to join this militant fragment with the blessing of my family.

With the kind of training I had and the life I lived, you end up one of two ways: You either become a lunatic, fanatical believer like the 9/11 terrorists and al Qaeda, who kill thinking Allah is pushing them to. Or, with all this training and killing, the religious zeal evaporates, and nothing is left but a fighting machine.

For me, it was the latter. It was strange—despite all those teachings, the faith and feelings disappeared. I became very cold. Life meant nothing whatsoever to me. I accepted that I wouldn't reach my twentieth year because I'd be killed before then. When life means nothing to you and you believe you won't survive except by killing, you know nothing else to do but keep killing.

The war environment affected me profoundly. I was rigid. There's not much room for flexibility in that life. For instance, if you say something, you'd better do it. Once you go back on your word, you're dead. It's a sign of weakness. Whatever you say goes, even if you're wrong. There was never a time that I said something and didn't do it. This built my reputation and strength, which enabled me to become a regimental leader. Other warriors will respect and follow you when you're like this. You could order a man to jump off a cliff, and he'd do it immediately.

As a warrior, every time you returned from the battlefield and other warriors witnessed that you'd dropped someone, they'd give you a point on your chart. Each point meant you were a stronger, better warrior, with more enemies killed. It was like the Second World War pilots who would paint decals on their planes of enemy aircraft they'd shot down. When we'd return from the battlefield, they'd say, "Zach dropped a few more." According to my chart, I ended up with 223 points.

The Daring American

In 1975 I had a divine encounter that changed my life. By that time the civil war had calmed down somewhat. There were cars and taxis in the streets, and people could go to work, school, and the market. One day I was bored. No school, no job, and no fights. I went to see a movie, but the film was dull, so I left. To reach my bus stop, I'd have to turn left from the theater. For some reason I turned right.

I saw a gathering at the corner and, thinking it was a fight, I rushed over. A tall American man was talking to the crowd. The very idea of an American talking publicly on the streets of Beirut was outrageous. "He's lucky I don't draw my knife and stab him," I thought.

He was a Southern Baptist missionary. I wasn't interested in what he had to say, so I began walking away. Suddenly I heard him say in Arabic with a Jordanian accent (with which I was very familiar), "Jesus Christ will give you hope, salvation, and a new life."

I stood rigid like a nail. He had used the word *Yasū* (Arabic for "Jesus"), which I'd never heard before. I knew Christians existed, but who was this *Yasū*? Was there really any new life, like he claimed? Was there salvation? Was there hope? I thought if this American was daring enough to stand on the streets of Beirut and make a statement like that, then he must know what he's talking about. So I decided to ask him.

"Do you believe in what you're saying?"

"Well, yes," he said. "Otherwise I wouldn't be standing here saying it."

"Explain it to me," I said.

This guy with the Jordanian accent began talking about Christ, but I interrupted him. "Hold it," I said. "I don't believe that your Christ exists—not in my life, at least. I can prove that your Christ doesn't exist in my life."

"Go ahead," the missionary said.

I related an event that happened during fighting several months before. I was returning from the battlefield with two warriors, one girl and one boy, when we were ambushed. As I took cover behind some rocks, the girl was with me, but the boy wasn't. I looked over the rocks and saw that he was down, injured but still alive. The girl decided to help him. I refused.

She looked at me strangely, then readied her machine gun, jumped over the rocks and walked toward the boy while shouting and shooting at the others. Reaching him and grabbing him by the shoulder, she started pulling him back, still shouting and shooting.

I decided I should help, so I did the same thing. I jumped out and started shooting and pulling until we were several feet from the rocks. The girl then tumbled over me, and I grabbed her and the guy and threw them behind the rocks.

The guy was already dead. The girl's eyes were flickering, her mouth was wide open, and blood was streaming from her jacket. I opened it and saw a wound the size of my fist in her side. I calmly drew my pistol and shot her dead. Then I flipped out.

I grabbed her machine gun and mine and jumped out—shooting and charging. I was crazy. The ambushers were sitting next to land mines. One of my bullets hit a land mine, detonating it and killing many of them. I was hit in the forehead with shrapnel and knocked unconscious. Passersby found me and carried me to the hospital, where I awoke later on.

So I asked the missionary, "If your Christ exists and is just, why did the girl have to die? I mean, it was I who refused to help."

The guy looked at me and asked two questions that shook me: "Why didn't you die? Why were you the only one to return alive?"

He shocked me. I suddenly remembered all the times during the four years of my fighting life that I was the only survivor. It had happened many times. I often returned bashed and injured, but alive.

I didn't want to talk to that man anymore. He really bothered me. I turned and walked away without a good-bye, nothing at all—which is an insult in the Middle East. But he was a real soul-winner. He dashed up behind me, pushed his card over my shoulder, and said, "Call me whenever you want." I pocketed his card and walked away.

That night I sat at the edge of my bed, unable to sleep, my head between my hands, the missionary's words repeating in my brain.

Appointment With *Yasū*

The next day I went to my part-time job at a printing house. I was working at an old machine when it suddenly jammed and stopped. I stared at it but heard and saw nothing because the missionary's words were playing in my head. The foreman came over and hit my shoulder to wake me up. That made me angry and I beat him up.

I then went home, got my pistol, and returned, intending to kill the foreman. But I stood there instead and asked myself, "OK, Zach, what are you going to do? You're going to shoot this man. He's going to fall and his blood will cover the ground. You've seen enough blood in your life. Why don't you go out, call that American guy, and calm down."

So, strangely enough, I did. I called the missionary and said, "I've got a pistol—I could kill someone if you don't talk to me." He immediately started talking about Christ. When he reached the point that he said Christ died for me, I burst into tears. This was significant—you must understand, crying was the ultimate shame. For four years during my fighting life, I never cried. Whenever I was in pain, physically or emotionally, I would bite my lips, leaving marks, even making them bleed. I *never* cried. But in that moment I burst into real tears.

The missionary said, "Put down your pistol and come see me." He directed me where to go. I gave the pistol to an associate, then went straight to his house. He was waiting for me with a Lebanese Christian.

We sat down and talked for a long time. Then the Lebanese believer offered me a Bible and said, "Will you please bless us with a reading?" I opened the book, and the first verse I saw was Matthew 11:28, "Come to Me all you who are tired…and I will give you rest" (NCV).

I fell to my knees, crying, and prayed, "Christ, I don't know You. This is the first time I've heard about You. I'm a very bad boy—I've cheated, lied, stolen, committed adultery, and even killed people. I don't think I'll ever be a good boy again in my life. But I promise only one thing—I'll try. You change me. I surrender my heart and soul to You."

I left, went back and retrieved my pistol, and started walking beside the only best friend I'd had for years—the seashore. Lebanon's entire western border is the Mediterranean Sea. I walked by the sea and thought about what had happened to me. In less than twenty-four hours I had prayed and become a Christian.

I was digesting what was happening to me when I suddenly noticed that my hand was heavy. I was still carrying my pistol. I took one look at it and knew it was a doorway to evil. I didn't want it anymore. I threw it into the sea. From that moment on I was a free man! Praise God! I was two months away from my seventeenth birthday, but I was so burdened that I felt like an ancient, hundred-year-old warrior.

A Warrior Takes a Stand

The change in me started happening quickly and dramatically. I was brave enough to tell my parents on the second day I had become a Christian. Maybe that was because I came from a very tough background where death meant nothing to me, or maybe it was because I was a killing machine and thought I was indestructible, or maybe it was because the life I had led to that point had created a guy who didn't scare easily—I don't know the reason I could tell my family so quickly.

You see, in a traditional Islamic family, for someone to become a Christian is a big deal. My father took my small New Testament out of my hand, shredded it, and slapped me several times. He also stepped backward, probably thinking I was going to jump him. My mom was more spooked than my dad. She went knocking on neighbors' doors, saying, "Be careful for your sons because my son became a Christian."

Initially people didn't believe it. I mean, who *would* believe that a guy like me—a regimental leader in an Islamic faction, a cold killer—had become a Christian?

Persecution didn't come immediately—mostly because people didn't believe it at first. But even after it sank in with people that I'd become a Christian, they didn't take action immediately for one reason: who wanted to tangle with me? I hadn't lost my reputation—I could kill so easily and quickly it was unbelievable. Even when they decided I should be killed, they couldn't find even one warrior from my area to attack me. They had to recruit warriors from another area who didn't know me.

Finally one evening about thirteen men came to my house and said,

"We want you in the mosque." I said, "Fine," and I went. As soon as I walked in, I knew I was on trial. One guy stood to my right, one to my left. Three imams stood in front of me with a multitude of men behind them.

An imam asked, "Son, have you strayed?" Remember, I really didn't know anything about Christianity then, and whatever I knew about Islam basically had disappeared.

"What do you mean by 'strayed'?" I asked.

"It means you've left the religion of your fathers."

"Oh, if you mean, 'Did I become a Christian?' yes, I became a Christian."

So the guy drilled me. If you were there, you would have said he was the cleverest person in the world and I was the stupidest person in the world. Every time he would "win" an argument against me, all the Muslims behind him would shout those Islamic shouts.

Finally I felt like my head was about to explode, so I shouted. Everyone got quiet. I looked at the imam very sternly and said, "Look, maybe what you're saying, thinking, and believing is right, and maybe what I'm saying, thinking, and believing is wrong. But there has been something planted in my heart. Not you—not ten people like you—and not any force in the whole universe can shift me out of it. Do whatever you want to me."

He excommunicated me. In Islam that means several things. First, if I'm married or to be married, then a divorce paper will be issued right away. Second, my civic identity is erased; it's as if I don't exist anymore—there are no documents, no papers, nothing. Third, my Muslim family will disinherit me. Fourth, if I don't become a Muslim again in three days, I will be killed.

"Who cares," I said in response to the imam.

That night at the trial was the turning point in my life as a Christian. The moment that caused me to grow up as a Christian was established that night because when I walked out of the mosque I got the worst beating of my life. The men from the mosque beat me unconscious. People had to carry me home.

No Price Too High

When I awoke, I questioned the truth more seriously. "Why is it Christ, not Muhammad?" I asked myself. "Why is it the Bible, not the Quran? Why is it Christianity, not Islam?"

So I went and bought myself a Quran. Remember, I came from a clergy family, and we had all kinds of Qurans in the house. But that day I wanted a book that no one had touched but me. I read it to try to find God. Trust me, if I'd found God in that book, I would've gone back to being a Muslim.

So, as a new Christian, I actually read the Quran before I read the Bible. And doing so changed my life. Here's why. The Quran uses very high Arabic. Experts will tell you that only one in every fifty thousand Arabs can read the Quran and tell you what it says. Because the Quran quotes the story of Christ from the Bible, and because of the specificity of the language, it's easy to prove from the Quran that Christ is God. That's why reading the Quran turned my attention to Christ more than the Bible did, initially.

So that's how God got hold of me. Since then I've been on an interesting journey. In the first twenty years after my conversion, eighteen attempts were made on my life—even some by my own family. I've been shot, stabbed, and beaten multiple times. Even since I immigrated to the West, I've been surrounded by Muslim mobs and attacked; but miraculously, I'm still here to share my testimony.

To Christians who think my testimony is amazing, I would say this: all the wounds I've suffered are normal to me. Unfortunately, pampered Christians in the West often forget there is a price tag in Christianity. If you aren't willing to pay the price, then the "clothes" you get might look sloppy on you.

To Muslims I would say this: anything you'll suffer for becoming a Christian is a very small price to pay for at least knowing where you're headed. Because without Jesus one day you'll stand before God, and then you'll find you've lost everything—both here and in the afterlife. So, in the name of Christ, I call you to the real light. Don't hesitate. No matter what, the price is not too high! All these wounds on earth are a small price for the freedom and peace I have in Christ. In heaven I'll have a very great reward. I hope we meet there.

Zachariah Anani is a former Sunni-Muslim Lebanese militia fighter. After he gave his life to Jesus, he became an evangelist and sought refuge in Canada. He has toured and spoken extensively on Islam and Christianity, sharing his miraculous conversion story in churches, at universities, and with a variety of media outlets. Numerous attempts have been made on his life by radical Muslims since his conversion. Undaunted, Zachariah continues to share the gospel of Jesus Christ with anyone who will listen. For more information, write ananizachariah@hotmail.com. To view medical documentation, see Appendix.

19

Jesus and the Atheist

The LORD is with you while you are with Him.
If you seek Him, He will be found by you;
but if you forsake Him, He will forsake you.

2 CHRONICLES 15:2

MY NAME IS Libby Baron. I was born in Hungary in 1962. Being raised on Marxist principles, I believed only in Darwinism and the theory of evolution. I didn't really know about God's existence until I was twenty-five, even though I had a supernatural experience with God when I was about seven. Here is what happened:

I developed a high fever and died. I reached heaven and was told to go back and share the experience and tell all people about the serenity, love, and peace that heaven offers. I didn't want to leave that place of complete contentment and acceptance, but my mission was to remind the world to "love one another; as I [God] have loved you" (John 13:34).

As a bonus, I was told I'd never have a high fever again—and I haven't. I also never needed more than three hours of sleep per night until my early forties. I sleep four to five hours these days. I feel energetically recharged each time I help someone and during times of fasting and prayer.

Unfortunately, living under Communism for so long left me with only vague memories of my childhood encounter, and the contemporary world of sin crawled into my life, slowly but surely, until it consumed me completely. Thankfully the Lord eventually intervened and did several miracles in my life to bring me into a relationship with Himself.

I was in my midtwenties when my mom was diagnosed with cancer. The doctors said it was incurable. It started in her thigh and spread from there. After a couple of unsuccessful surgeries, we knew we were losing her. She was preparing to go for her third surgery, but we just saw a body that was wasting away in the hospital bed. We said good-bye to her before the surgery, as she cried inconsolably.

The next day was the surgery. She survived it, and they brought her back into her room to recover. My brother is a doctor and he'd found the best doctors for her, but no one guaranteed us anything—except that she was going to die.

It took a while until she was able to speak again, but when she could, she told us that the night before the surgery she had a vision of Jesus, and He spoke with her. That was the first time I'd heard the name "Jesus." (See chapter 32 "From Communism to Christ" by Maria Baron.)

My parents were very active in the Communist Party. My mom was a teacher and my dad an engineer. To have those kinds of jobs in that society, you had to publicly deny God. Before you were hired, there was a meeting with a committee of employers who intensely interviewed you. The question asked was, "Do you believe in God?" The answer to give was always, "No." The reasons were obvious: you had a family and you had to live.

In my case, when I was publicly interviewed, I was already twenty-two. I answered "No" for only one reason: I genuinely didn't believe. The very idea of God's existence was laughable to me at that time in my life. The way you were raised under Communism brainwashed you into thinking that any belief in God would steer you away from your goal in life.

I started seeking God when my mom first mentioned Jesus, and when I saw the way she viewed Him and spoke to Him. If someone you love and are close to is talking that seriously about God, it causes you to question your beliefs. Witnessing the profound change in her, not to mention the fact that she survived the cancer the doctors said there was no hope for, was eye-opening for me. Her surgery was more than twenty-five years ago, and, praise God, my mom is over seventy-five years old today! God touched my whole family by curing her.

Right after she was cured, my mom said, "I cannot go back to work anymore. I cannot chase kids away from church. I cannot chase families away from going and praising God." That was part of her job as

89

a schoolteacher in Hungary. So she quit her job and never went to the school again.

She started attending the same Orthodox church on the corner that she'd chased kids and families away from. My father eventually found Jesus through a Christian neighbor who invited him to a Baptist church, where he was also baptized. For the last five years of his life my father told me about the happiness he had in his life after meeting Jesus. I wasn't ready to hear it yet, but he was trying to tell me. It wasn't until he died that our loving heavenly Father consoled me once again. Losing my father was the most painful time in my life. He meant everything to me. He was my hero, and I was his sunshine.

On the day of my father's funeral I had a vision of Jesus Christ. God spoke to me and said, "This is the path I have for you." By that time I'd already immigrated to the United States and had lived here for years. After the funeral I flew back to America and started looking for a church near my home in Queens, New York. I visited quite a few, and then I was invited to one church where the pastor's message seemed to be tailored just for me. The amazing thing was, the preacher looked exactly like my dad's friend—that Christian neighbor who had originally invited him to the Baptist church where my dad found Jesus and got baptized! The preacher and my dad's friend could have been brothers! It was shocking to me, but I knew it was a sign from God.

With each word the man spoke, it was like my father was speaking to me. I broke into tears and admitted that my life was nothing but sin and lies—I didn't want any part of my old life anymore. I wanted to end everything right there and just let Jesus Christ lead me. I was home. I gave my life to Jesus and was baptized, and have grown so much in my walk with Him since then.

God has given me compassion for others, and today He leads me to pray for people regularly wherever I am. I often see them miraculously healed and set free. My mom was baptized a year after me. In August 2012 my sixteen-year-old daughter came to know Jesus and was baptized as well. I have come to know with certainty that Jesus is real, and He loves you so much.

 **Libby Baron** is a schoolteacher in New York City and lives with her family in Queens, New York. For more information, write libarvi@gmail.com.

20

The E-Mail From God

And we know that all things work together
for good to those who love God, to those who
are the called according to His purpose.

ROMANS 8:28

*M*Y NAME IS Anton Stubbs. I was born in 1973 and raised
in Queens, New York. I graduated from St. John's University in Jamaica,
New York, where I earned a bachelor's degree in marketing. After college
I worked for a while in the academic and business worlds before deciding
finally to pursue my childhood dream of becoming a US Marine. Today
I'm a former captain in the US Marine Corps. I survived two combat
tours to Iraq, where I believe God's hand of protection was on me, and
I experienced several divine interventions. I returned from my second
tour to Iraq in 2005, and currently reside with my wife and three children in Virginia.

I grew up attending a nondenominational, evangelical Christian
church, and from the time I was very young I have experienced some
great things in God. My parents always encouraged me to have a personal relationship with God. They sang in the choir, and I was involved
in youth ministry and Sunday school. When I was fourteen, I decided to
accept the lordship of Jesus Christ and serve Him. Throughout the course
of my youth I knew God to be real through my experiences. I always felt
God's presence, whether it was feeling the move of the Holy Spirit in a
church service or in my living room.

When I was in Iraq I experienced several divine interventions in
which I believe God protected me. When you're in a combat environment,

92

those experiences, I have found, are numerous. One incident in particular stands out to me as miraculous.

During my second tour in Iraq, I served with the 1st Marine Division G4 Supply as a supply expert on the commanding general's staff. My job was to support our units spread across the Al Anbar province, which is roughly the size of North Carolina. I communicated with our units and supply officers mainly through phone and e-mail. I provided them support and guidance, and there were many occasions when I went out to their locations in hostile environments to assist them personally.

This specific incident happened around midday. I was communicating back and forth via e-mail with a supply officer. He had some issues, and I was trying to help him. When I finished with him, I decided to take a break. I was going to head back to my living quarters, which we called "hooches." This particular camp in Ramadi was built around one of Saddam Hussein's old palaces, so I was indoors in a protected area. I was going to leave that protected area and walk across an open field to my living quarters. It was only a few minutes' walk.

As I was finishing up on the computer, I had to go to the bathroom. I began to pack up my gear, put on my helmet and flak jacket, grab my weapon, and head for the Port-a-Johns, which were in front of the quarters. As I was getting my gear on and was just about to leave, another e-mail popped up. I really had to go, but thought, "OK, let me look at this e-mail real quick." I put my gear down, went to the computer, looked at the e-mail, and started typing a little bit. Suddenly I heard a barrage of mortar explosions outside. In that area of Ramadi we got daily attacks, and I could tell the rounds had come in close and right together—*boom! boom! boom!*

"Wow! That was pretty close!" I thought. But we were used to it, so I didn't give it too much thought beyond that. I finished with the computer, sent my e-mail, and by then *really* had to use the bathroom.

I packed up my gear and walked out of the palace. I could see smoke rising from where the Port-a-Johns and hooches were (about sixty-five yards away). As I approached, I saw that the Port-a-Johns had been destroyed. The mortar rounds had directly hit the Port-a-Johns and hooches, destroying that whole area. There were several casualties. The whole scene was shocking to me, because had I not answered that last e-mail I would've been in the Port-a-Johns, probably right when the rounds came in. I praise the Lord that He spared me that day.

So many times we find ourselves running late for something, diverted from our intended path, and we really never know what God is doing. He may be saving us from an accident or some other danger about which we are unaware. God knows the big picture. He sees everything that happens. We need to trust Him and know that He's looking out for us.

I know a guy who worked in the World Trade Center and was late to work on September 11, 2001, when the towers were hit. Because he was running late, he wasn't in the towers when they were attacked, and he's alive today to tell the story. Many other people have stories that involve incidents like that.

In the combat zone they're frequent. There were probably times when I was saved and didn't even know it. The mortar attack is an example of one instance when I know I would have been destroyed had I been hit. I saw the extent of the damage to the Port-a-Johns and the surrounding area—they were full of holes like Swiss cheese. If that wasn't a divine intervention, I don't know what is. I'm very thankful to the Lord for preserving my life.

If you don't believe in God or are struggling with doubt, I would say to you that God is real. He loves you. He loves us all so much. The Bible says, "For God so loved the world that He gave His only begotten Son, that whoever believes in Him should not perish but have everlasting life" (John 3:16). All you have to do, according to the Bible, is "confess with your mouth the Lord Jesus and believe in your heart that God has raised Him from the dead, [and] you will be saved" (Rom. 10:9).

It's that simple. But that's just the beginning. That puts you on the road to learn more about who Jesus is, who God is, and what your role is in this life. It's an amazing adventure.

Anton Stubbs is a former captain in the US Marine Corps. He and his wife and three children live in Virginia. For more information, write antonstubbs@aol.com.

21

The Golden Fish

O LORD, You have searched me and known
me....And are acquainted with all my ways.

PSALM 139:1, 3

*M*Y NAME IS Eric Metaxas. In 1988, near my twenty-fifth
birthday, I had a life-changing dream in which God spoke to me in what
I've called "the secret vocabulary of my heart." In order for that dream
to make sense, I'll have to reveal that vocabulary. If you had examined
my life back then, you probably would have concluded there were three
things at the heart of my identity: (1) being Greek; (2) fishing; and (3) the
search for meaning and the life of the mind.

My dad is Greek and my mother German. They met in an English
class in Manhattan in 1956. I was born in 1963 and attended a Greek
Orthodox parochial school through fourth grade. In 1972 we moved to
Danbury, Connecticut, where I attended public school and went to Greek
church every Sunday.

For Greek Americans, being Greek is hugely important. Perhaps
because I'm half Greek, it was especially important for my dad to communicate this to me. Once when he saw a chrome fish on a bumper he
explained that this was from the Greek word *ixthys*, meaning "fish." The
early Christians used it as an acronym: Iesus Xristos THeos Ymon Sotir,
"Jesus Christ Son of God Our Savior." It was their secret symbol.

My only hobby besides watching TV was fishing, which I did a lot of.
During college at Yale, I was exposed to the life of the mind, and I half-
heartedly attempted to divine the meaning of life, with mixed results. I
never believed our lives are meaningless, but neither did I settle on any
particular alternative.

Sometime after graduation I came up with a kind of answer, involving the symbolic image of drilling through ice on the surface of a lake. It was a vaguely Jungian/Freudian idea that said the goal of life and all religions was to drill through this ice, which represented the conscious mind, in order to touch the water beneath, which represented Jung's "collective unconscious," a vague "God force" that somehow connected all humanity. It was an Eastern and impersonal idea of God, making no particular claims on anyone. How one went about doing any of this was anybody's guess.

Graduation was like stepping off the ladder I'd been climbing my whole life. At Yale I majored in English, edited the humor magazine, and sang in some musicals. At graduation I was Class Day speaker, preceding the main speaker—my future friend Dick Cavett—and I received several awards for my short fiction. What could lie ahead but success?

Instead I was launched into a stepless void, unable to climb toward what I thought I'd wanted to achieve, which was success as a fiction writer. I sold some humor pieces to the *Atlantic*, and got in to two elite writers' colonies, but wrote almost no fiction. I lived in Boston for two years and clung to a sad relationship. One might say I floated and drifted, which led to that humiliating cul-de-sac of moving back in with one's parents.

That was a painful time. My now long-distance relationship was floundering, and I took the only job I could get then, proofreading chemical manuals at Union Carbide's world headquarters. My cubicle was a quarter mile from the nearest window. (And the password was...Gehenna.)

But it was there, in the belly of the corporate whale, that I would finally consider the question of God. In my misery I befriended a graphic designer, who began engaging me on this issue. Ed was older, married with kids, and one of those born-again Christians I'd been trained at Yale to steer well clear of. I was wary, but in my pain I was desperate enough to keep the conversation going—for months. But whenever Ed invited me to church, I demurred.

One day, Ed said, "Perhaps you don't really know God as well as you think, Eric." I was offended. Anyone with a brain knew that even if God existed, we certainly couldn't *know* it, and we'd just have to content ourselves with agnosticism. But I wasn't content. Ed told me to pray that God would reveal Himself to me, but praying to a God I wasn't sure existed didn't make sense. In my confusion, however, I sometimes did ask for a sign.

Things changed in June 1988; my uncle had a stroke and went into a coma. Ed said he and some friends were praying for him. I was astounded at this kindness and at the idea that these people believed God heard our prayers. A few days later Ed asked if he could pray for my uncle with me. I followed him into a fluorescent-lit conference room. I'd never done anything like this, but I closed my eyes and something transcendent seemed to occur, as though a window had opened into another realm, and I felt the faintest touch of some heavenly breeze. When it was over, I opened my eyes, wondering, "What was that?"

Around this time a slight shift was happening in my mind too. I'd picked up M. Scott Peck's *People of the Lie*, and this Harvard psychologist's experiences with evil got my attention. If real evil existed, did God exist too? I was also reading Thomas Merton's *The Seven Storey Mountain* and Dietrich Bonhoeffer's *Cost of Discipleship*, though I cannot remember if I was reading these before or after the dream.

Ah, yes, the dream.

Around my twenty-fifth birthday I dreamed I was ice fishing on Candlewood Lake in Danbury, Connecticut. I looked into the large hole we'd cut in the ice and saw a fish's snout poking out. Of course, this never actually happens. I picked it up by the gills and held it up. It was a large pickerel or pike. In the dazzlingly bright sunlight shining through the blue sky and off the white snow onto the bronze-colored fish, it appeared golden. But then I realized it didn't merely look golden, it actually *was* golden. It was a living, golden fish, as if I were in a fairytale.

Suddenly I understood that this golden fish was *IXTHYS*—Jesus Christ the Son of God Our Savior—and I knew God was one-upping me in the language of my own symbol system. I'd wanted to touch inert water, to touch the so-called collective unconscious, but He had something more: this was His Son, a living person, Jesus Christ. I realized in the dream that He was real and had come from the other side and now I was holding Him there in the bright sunlight and at long last my search was over. I was flooded with joy.

When I went to work the next day, I told Ed about the dream. And I said what I never would've said before—and would've cringed to hear anyone else say—"I've accepted Jesus." When I spoke those words I was flooded with the same joy I experienced inside the dream. I've had that joy with me ever since.

 **Eric Metaxas** is the author of the *New York Times* best seller *Bonhoeffer*, the best seller *Amazing Grace: William Wilberforce and the Heroic Campaign to End Slavery*, and more than thirty other books. He is currently the voice of *BreakPoint*, a commentary broadcast on fourteen hundred radio outlets nationwide to an audience of eight million. He was the keynote speaker at the 2012 National Prayer Breakfast in Washington DC, and was awarded the Canterbury Medal in 2011 by the Becket Fund for Religious Freedom. Eric has written for *VeggieTales*, Chuck Colson, and the *New York Times*. He lives in New York with his wife and daughter. For more information, write eric@ericmetaxas.com or visit www.EricMetaxas.com.

22

Stepping Out in Faith

Trust in the LORD with all your heart, and
lean not on your own understanding;
in all your ways acknowledge Him,
and He shall direct your paths.

PROVERBS 3:5–6

MY NAME IS Denise Lotierzo-Block. I was born in Brooklyn,
New York, in 1959. I graduated college with an accounting degree, then
joined my dad in his accounting firm on Long Island, New York.

I was raised Catholic but made my own decision to follow Jesus
during college. When my husband, Gary, and I had our daughter,
Melanie, we began attending a Lutheran church, where we've been
since the early 1990s.

I experienced an incredible miracle that really strengthened my faith.
It was the first Saturday in February 2002. Gary was seeing a client, and
Melanie and I were preparing to leave for breakfast. We had a little
beagle that liked to sleep on the stairs. I was descending the stairs, and
usually I'd say, "Get down!" and she'd move. That day she was slightly
slow, I was slightly fast, we got tangled, and I fell down about six steps.
The next thing I knew, I was at the bottom of the steps, feeling like my
head was exploding. I knew something was *really* wrong, because that
was the most excruciating pain I'd ever felt.

Melanie ran and got our neighbor Diane, who came over and called
an ambulance. They carried me to the ambulance on a stretcher, and the
EMT said, "Tell me if you feel like vomiting."

I thought, "I hurt my head; why would I throw up?" But no sooner
had she said that than I started heaving. I threw up for almost *seven days.*

The EMTs called Gary, who met us at the hospital. Diane followed the ambulance with my daughter. When we arrived, Diane called and asked someone from the church to start praying. That person called someone else, and so on; there was lots of prayer happening.

A CT scan was performed, and eventually a doctor came in, wringing his hands, saying, "I have terrible news." He said I had a traumatic brain injury, with bleeding in the brain, called a subdural hematoma. The dura is the protective skin surrounding the brain. I basically had a hemorrhage on my brain. The scan showed my brain being concave from all the blood pooling in it, which usually causes brain damage.

He continued, "You need brain surgery." I wasn't really understanding. I looked at Gary, and his head was in his arms. Gary's pretty strong—I knew it was serious for him to be like that.

After that I remember lying there and vomiting about every two minutes. Many people visited: friends, family, my pastor. I later learned they'd brought in one of the best brain surgeons in New York for me. God was working there too.

At one point the brain surgeon, the neurosurgeon, and the anesthesiologist came to see me. They explained how they were going to open my skull. That was freaky. I was *terrified*. I didn't want to leave my child or husband. The pain was horrible. I couldn't imagine how I didn't die from that much pain. I didn't know the human body could register that level of pain, and that you could live through it. I had a *baby*. *That* was pain. This made childbirth seem like a cakewalk. It was awful.

Before they operate, you're put in another room where your family can come to talk with you, presumably in case they never see you again. My family and friends were in the room, along with our friend Gary, from church, who prayed over me.

Everybody was crying because the doctors had said, "Look, this is the deal: You have a subdural hematoma. We must operate. There's a good chance you won't survive. We're sorry, but we have to tell you this. If you do survive, you could be paralyzed and/or brain damaged."

That's what you go in with. Death would've been preferable, possibly, to brain damage or paralysis. I'm not sure. All I know is that I was petrified. I didn't want anyone going into my brain; my brain and I were good friends and I liked it just as it was.

Here's the miraculous part of the story. After our friend Gary prayed over me, I had the most unbelievable sense of peace that I'd ever felt in my life. Unlike anything before or since. It wasn't like God said, "You'll be OK." He didn't. It was that I was thinking whatever way it went, I was totally fine with it. I knew I could die, and I was OK with it, knowing that I felt God and had His peace that surpasses understanding. It was other-worldly and supernatural. It's the peace the Bible describes in Philippians 4:7 and John 14:27.

My situation wasn't good, and through all that agony, as I was watching my friends and family crying, I was totally at peace. That was the miracle. I realized that whatever happened, God had it covered. It was amazing. I don't think even the fact that I survived compared with the feeling that God was in control. Right then I totally surrendered my life and the whole situation to God, saying, "Your will be done." That was the first time I had ever done that. I totally relied on God.

I went into the operating room with pain but no fear. I survived the surgery. I don't remember this, but my surgeon told me that when I started coming to in recovery, he asked, "Do you have any questions?"

I said, "When can I ski?" He said when he heard that, he knew I'd be OK. It was February, and my mind was on the ski trips we'd planned. I spent eight days in ICU. I was still vomiting. There was tremendous pain, but I had good medication.

I eventually came home. It was a long recovery. A month after the accident our friend Chris was having his fiftieth birthday party at a coffee house, and I went. I was only planning to stay an hour because I couldn't sit up for long—my head still hurt badly. And I was on *heavy-duty* medication.

My pastor was there, and he asked me to play chess with him. I sat down to play, but I couldn't think the moves through. That was my first indication something was wrong.

My post-op was several days later. I said to my surgeon, "I was trying to play chess, and I couldn't."

"Well, you aren't the same person you were a month ago," he answered. That statement freaked me out.

"What do you mean?"

"You won't be able to do the things you used to," he said.

I couldn't believe it! Gradually I started noticing there were things I couldn't do. I couldn't read. I had difficulty speaking. It was embarrassing; I'd start talking and get all jammed up. I couldn't say some words, such as *spoon*. I knew what I wanted to say, I knew what a spoon was, but the word wouldn't come out of my mouth. Sometimes I could even spell the word but couldn't say it.

The reading problem was the worst because we're a family of readers. The best gift you can give someone in my family is a book. I have floor to ceiling bookshelves in my house. I couldn't read, and that was devastating.

I went to cognitive rehabilitation, but the only thing that was good for was trying to get me to accept my limitations. I wasn't OK with that, so I became a cognitive-rehab dropout. I stopped going and didn't read for almost two years. It was depressing and difficult. It seemed like I retained everything I knew before the accident, but everything after the accident I couldn't remember.

There was one novel that I'd really enjoyed. One day I stepped out in faith, saying, "I'm going to take this book and start a book club for Christian women." I said, "God, I believe You can heal me, if You want to. I'm starting a book club, although I can't read." I leaned on God's Word—in particular Proverbs 3:5–6: "Trust in the LORD with all your heart, and lean not on your own understanding; in all your ways acknowledge Him, and He shall direct your paths." I was walking by faith, not trying to understand everything.

I got about ten women together with this book and started a book discussion and tea group at my home. It was fabulous. Everyone loved it. My friend Jen proposed a book for the next meeting. It was a thin book. Everyone knew I couldn't read, so one of the girls got me the book on tape, and I bought the book itself.

At night after dinner I'd listen to the book on tape and would try to follow along and read just one page. The next day I'd try to read the same page from the day before, and the next page. Then I'd listen to it. I did this for the entire book. I got the general idea of the book. Although I couldn't remember details, I was able to somewhat discuss it at the next meeting.

After that I started with Arthur Rimbaud, the French poet. I have it in French and English. I'd try to read a page in English, and a page in French, every night. From there I just started reading! I was praying the whole time, and I believe my ability to read was a gift from God. I wanted it so badly and asked Him fervently, "Please, Lord, let me read again."

He answered my prayers—today I'm reading! It took more than two years, but I'm reading again! My speech and language returned also. I still get confused sometimes in times of stress, but I'm about 99 percent recovered, and I'm back to work full time. It's really a miracle, considering that the doctors weren't sure if I'd even survive. My brain surgeon says I'm a miracle. God still performs miracles!

Denise Lotierzo-Block lives with her husband on Long Island, New York, where she works as an accountant in her family's accounting firm. Denise and her husband have one grown daughter. For more information, write DeniseLotierzo@gmail.com or visit www.lotierzocpa.com. To view medical documentation, see Appendix.

23

From Demon Possession and Rebellion to Deliverance and Love

Rebellion is as the sin of witchcraft.

1 Samuel 15:23

*M*Y NAME IS Kevin Frohlich. My wife and I are Christian missionaries in Malaysia, but there was a time when I didn't believe in Christ. I grew up with a lust for evil and the occult that led me down a path of self-destruction. I surely would have spent an eternity in hell if not for God's intervention.

I was born in Rhodesia (now Zimbabwe), Africa, in 1968. When I was a baby, my parents divorced, and my mother and I went to live with my grandparents. During that time I started having supernatural experiences and developing a "psychic power." I was able to see demonic entities in my room—huge, black silhouettes. At age four I started talking to them, confiding in them, and seeing them as my only friends. This led me to become a bitter, withdrawn, lonely child; I didn't play much with other kids. These "things" would tell me many lies, like that I wasn't loved. I also had many dreams of death and destruction and was always fearful.

At the same time my mother started practicing "automatic writing." She would sit in a dark room with candles and speak with spirits. They would pick her hand up and write as a form of witchcraft or divination. This opened many doors for evil to attack us. The spirits tried to make my mom commit suicide. She tried many times to stab herself to death (unsuccessfully, thank God). She would go into a trance, run down the hallway, and ram her head into the wall trying to break her neck. My mother was able to hear the spirits, but she could never see them. I, unfortunately, was able to see them. These hideous-looking creatures tormented me constantly in my room.

Things worsened, and at one point they made me ill. I ended up in the hospital with a high temperature that the doctors couldn't bring down. They couldn't determine what was wrong. I came very close to death. Praise God, I survived. I believe it was a demonic illness because none of the tests revealed anything, but I miraculously recovered. I have an uncle who is a born-again believer, and he was praying for our family. I am sure his prayers affected my recovery.

Eventually we moved to South Africa, where I became very rebellious—stealing, smoking, and drinking. In high school I wouldn't bother to study. I got into the heavy metal music scene, which I really enjoyed. Through that culture, I was introduced to marijuana and other drugs.

When I went off to university in Johannesburg, I grew my hair long and began smoking weed often, drinking, partying, and carrying on a dysfunctional life. I started realizing that every time I listened to heavy metal music, I'd go into a demonic trance—the same kind my mother would go into when those "things" used to possess her and try to kill her.

I would do hideous things while in the trances. I would cut myself with a scalpel and write "666" on the wall of my room with my blood under the control of this demonic influence. I would draw pictures in blood and write curses to people in blood. When I would go into a trance, sometimes I would look in the mirror and see a demonic image that would communicate with me. It would tell me things, such as what was happening in my hometown. I would tell my friends what the demons said, and they'd laugh—until they would hear about it several days later from their families back home.

I was nicknamed "Psycho." People were frightened of me, and I don't blame them, because I was weird. I had these so-called powers that these demonic spirits were giving me. I could read people's minds and manipulate people through thoughts.

As time passed, I began to have very scary experiences that I couldn't control. One night I was lying in bed and something grabbed my foot and started physically shaking my leg. I was trying to force myself not to go into a demonic trance so I could avoid seeing what had grabbed me. When I turned onto my side, the cord to my bedside lamp actually started tapping on the table.

On another occasion I felt an evil presence come into my bedroom, and I became pinned to my bed. I was fully awake but could not move. I was not on drugs; I hadn't been for a long time at that point. I saw a red-eyed demon begin to manifest in my room. I somehow knew it was coming to kill me. I struggled desperately to free myself from whatever was pinning me down, and I finally was able to get up. I ran to my closet and found an old Bible lying among my shoes. It had been given to me as a kid.

I picked up the Bible, put it against my heart, and cried out, "God, if You're out there, please help me!" I climbed out the bedroom window and down the gutters of my house, and smoked several cigarettes to calm myself. After a while I returned to my bedroom, but I left the light on all night, clutching the Bible against my chest. I awoke in the morning after having the most peaceful night's sleep I'd ever had.

Many more crazy things transpired. I eventually sought help from Pastor Malcolm Hurter in Ermelo, South Africa. He led me in the sinner's prayer to accept Jesus. We burned all my heavy metal posters, and my drug and occult paraphernalia. Then he and his team prayed with me for about twelve hours, literally performing an exorcism and casting multiple demons out of me.

I knew I was being influenced by spirits, but I didn't realize they were inside me—I was actually possessed. It was a tremendous battle; those demons didn't want to leave. Eventually I was cleansed by the blood of Christ. A warm, loving feeling gushed through my body, and the most amazing sense of peace enveloped me. Jesus's love was so great, and I was a broken man, crying like a baby. God did such a miraculous work in me that night that when I later saw my father, he looked at me and asked four times, "Kevin, my son, is this you?" My countenance had changed drastically because of Jesus's love and all the stuff from which I'd been delivered. It was incredible!

Since that day I've been wholeheartedly following Christ. He has led my family and me to mission fields across the world, from Asia to the Middle East, proclaiming His gospel. If you don't know the Lord, cry out to Him and say, "Lord, if You're real, show Yourself to me." If you're honestly seeking Him, He will reveal Himself to you, just as He did for me.

 **Kevin Frohlich** is currently serving as a full-time missionary with the international Youth With A Mission ministry. He lives in Malaysia with his wife and children. Kevin's autobiography, *Rebellion Is as the Sin of Witchcraft*, tells the unabridged story of his remarkable deliverance from occult powers. For more information, visit www.lulu.com/spotlight/kevinfrohlich, or write KevinFrohlich@gmail.com.

24

Jesus, My Provider

What is man that You take thought of him,
and the son of man that You care for him?

PSALM 8:4, NAS

MY NAME IS Regine Paul Jones. I was born in Brooklyn, New York, in 1975 of Haitian ancestry, and grew up on Long Island. I've experienced many miracles, and I'd like to share one with you. I hope my testimony encourages you to know that God is real and He loves you.

During high school, my dream was to attend St. John's University in Queens, New York. My parents were doing well in Haiti with a ranch and several properties they owned. My dad also had a lucrative job. My parents would send my sister and me money for school and other things, as we were living with our aunt in New York.

During that time, there was much political unrest in Haiti. My parents' ranch was ransacked and looted. All their animals were either slaughtered or stolen. My father ended up in prison in Haiti, so all the money he had then was redirected and spent trying to free him. It was a very bad time.

Eventually time came for me to apply to college. I was accepted by St. John's and thought I was set. But with my father still in prison, the money wasn't flowing in like it had been for my family. It turned out that money wasn't put away for me like I thought. The door to my dream of attending St. John's was closed. I was devastated.

Because I had a B average I was able to attend any City University of New York school. But it was August, and I didn't have a plan B because I thought I was going to St. John's. At that late stage the only other options

109

open to me were Medgar Evers College in Brooklyn and York College in Queens. I chose York and was *so* mad at God.

I said, "How could You mock me like this? I'm in *Queens*, only a few blocks from St. John's! I'm not going to talk to *You* or *anybody*. I am going to come, sit in the cafeteria, eat a bagel, and do my work."

That lasted about three days. I started making friends and having fun. I met many young Christians who demonstrated a lifestyle that went along with their faith. I never had that modeled for me growing up, unfortunately. I was raised Catholic and thought you just accepted the Lord into your life and then you lived how you thought was best. At college I saw people really living for Jesus—reading the Bible every day and having fun. God was involved in their lives daily.

I felt God was telling me, "My plan for sending you here was to take you to the next level of knowing and understanding Me." I committed my life to the Lord Jesus Christ at age nineteen. I started singing in the choir, reading the Bible, and developing a relationship with the Lord. Having other young Christians I could talk and pray with was awesome. I matured in my faith. I stayed there two years, then God opened the door for me to fulfill my dream of attending St. John's, which was a *major* miracle.

I prayed, "Lord, I want to go to St. John's, but I have no money." My father was still in prison; I was in the same situation I had been in two years before. I felt like the Lord said, "I will send you to St. John's." By faith, I kept going. I was also given a prophetic word from an elder at church. She didn't know I wanted to attend St. John's, but while she was praying for me, she said, "I see a school in front of me. The Lord is telling me it's St. John's." Just thinking about that still gives me goose bumps!

"I don't know how that will happen," I thought. "I'll just trust the Lord."

I went to school one day at York and saw a woman who was in the Christian club with me. I told her I wanted to go to St. John's but that it seemed impossible because of my average. She smiled and said, "Is anything too hard for the Lord?"

I couldn't argue with her. I said, "I guess not." I needed a B in philosophy class, which would give me the 2.5 GPA I needed to transfer from York to St. John's. I ended up getting that grade, which was great, but I told God, "Lord, but that doesn't handle the financial issue." I thought maybe I should look at more classes at York, just to be on the safe side.

Then I began thinking that God would be insulted. If I believed He would send me to St. John's, then I should act that way. I felt it was almost a sin to look at York's fall school schedule to come up with a contingency plan, as if there was a possibility that God wouldn't come through.

I felt like God was saying, "If I told you I would do something, don't start making a plan B."

I said, "All right, Lord. You win." I never even looked at a program schedule for York; I started choosing my classes for St. John's.

Several weeks passed, and it was a couple days before I had to register for St. John's. I awoke that morning and heard the Lord say, "Go buy your notebooks for school."

I said, "Lord, I'd love to, but I have no money."

I went to do laundry and five dollars fell out of my pocket. I went to the ninety-nine cents store and bought notebooks with the money. The next day the Lord told me to go get my picture taken for my school ID and to go to orientation. So I went. Again, I had no idea how I was going to register for school.

The night before classes were to start, a woman called me at home and said, "Hi, this is St. John's University calling. Are you coming to school tomorrow?"

I said, "Honestly, I'm waiting to see what happens because my parents are trying to arrange the money for my tuition."

"Don't worry about that," she said. "Just come. A $3,500 grant came in for you."

I was in shock! I thought she surely must be mistaken because I never applied for a grant—my grades were too low. Then I thought that maybe it was the financial aid I had applied for. A friend of mine (who had the gift of prophecy) had said to me before that night, "The Lord told me you'll get $3,000 from somewhere." It was a week later the school called and told me about the grant!

The next day I went to school, thinking, "I'll go in faith. The school clearly made a mistake because I *never* applied for a grant." I walked into the financial aid office and said, "I understand that this grant is probably the financial aid I applied for."

"No, no," the woman said. "Give me your bursar bill." She took the paper, started crossing things out, and said, "This means your classes are all paid for, and this is your credit balance."

I had extra money in my account left over! I could buy books, lunch—anything I needed for school! I went in thinking I owed them money, and it turned out they *gave me* money! Every semester that I was able to go to school was a miracle. I graduated from St. John's in 1998 with a communications degree.

I praise God for His supernatural provision and guidance in my life! God really had a miraculous, faith-building way of dealing with me during that time. To this day I have no idea where that grant came from. I never applied for one!

Regine Paul Jones has been walking with Jesus for more than twenty years. She currently works in the pharmaceutical advertising industry, and resides with her husband in Delaware. For more information, write reginepjones@gmail.com.

25

Poisoned!

And these signs will follow those who believe:
In My name they will cast out demons; they
will speak with new tongues; they will take
up serpents; and if they drink anything
deadly, it will by no means hurt them.

MARK 16:17–18

Y NAME IS Mark Russak. I was born in 1959 in New Jersey and raised Catholic. I had a fairly strong childhood faith and talked to God regularly.

Growing up, I loved sports. I played baseball, basketball, or football almost daily. One day when I was around eleven years old, I played basketball aggressively for about an hour, working up a good sweat. I came home very thirsty.

Just before I arrived, my oldest brother had returned home from my grandmother's house. We were having plumbing problems in our house, so he'd gotten some industrial-strength drain cleaner from my grandmother for us. It was very strong, designed for large, severely clogged pipes. Unfortunately, its original container was leaking so my grandmother transferred it into a glass juice container, presumably thinking it would hold better.

She told my brother what it was, but he was coming in and out of the house, unloading packages from the car, and he'd put several of the containers on our dining room table just as I was coming in from playing basketball.

I saw a container with purple liquid and thought, "Grape juice!" In my sweat-covered state, I thought this was terrific. I poured myself a big glass of grape juice. Once I started drinking, I quickly realized it wasn't grape juice and spit it out. We had a lace tablecloth over our dining room table. I was standing over the table drinking; once I spit it out, I watched our tablecloth begin disappearing—literally burning away. I thought, "This isn't good," and got scared. I ran to the bathroom and saw that my skin was beginning to disintegrate. The cleaner was eating away my lip, tongue, and the roof of my mouth. I spit up as much as I could.

When I felt like I got as much out as possible, I found my mother in the den and said, "What's in the grape juice?"

One look at me and she screamed in horror. Off I went to Hackensack hospital.

After many tests and probing, they eventually determined everything was out of me and I was stabilized. When you spit liquid out, there's spritz in the air and, just as the tablecloth disintegrated, so did my clothes. I had holes in my shirt, sweatshirt, and dungarees. Everything this stuff touched just burned away. I later learned it had a sulfuric acid base (one of the stronger acids).

I developed a high-pitched voice. I could barely speak because the acid had gone down my throat. The staff said I'd be hospitalized for a week, minimum; more tests would be needed to assess the damage to my insides. The next day they said all my throat lining was burned away, and they'd wait for a little healing, but within the next few days they'd have to surgically remove my larynx (voice box). Everything was too raw and sensitive to do this immediately. Being about eleven years old, I was frightened but really didn't understand the magnitude of what was happening.

On day three the doctors said, "We must perform more tests because we're going to operate and remove your voice box." They took whatever type of X-rays were available then (this was 1969 or 1970) and returned to my bedside looking happy but perplexed. They informed my parents and me that somehow the burns in my esophagus and larynx had completely healed and surgery wasn't necessary.

My doctor said, "I don't understand this. It's nothing short of an absolute miracle." My mother made the sign of the cross and began weeping. My father had a big smile, thanking the doctors for their help. I stayed in the hospital several more days. My lip was still raw. For several weeks

I had to treat my tongue and lip with medication. I sounded like Mickey Mouse for a while, but eventually everything healed.

I don't particularly remember praying about this. I came to understand much later the significance of prayer, and I do believe my parents' prayers impacted what happened. I was too young then to understand it was a miracle. I was just grateful to be released from the hospital. After I got home, friends visited me. Naturally, they all brought grape juice! My mother thought that was horrific. From then on she never allowed grape juice in our house.

Although this miracle occurred when I was young, what happened more than twenty years later is what I cherish most. In the early 1990s I began attending a nondenominational, charismatic church. An older guy there befriended me and invited me to his home for a monthly group Bible study. I began attending, and at the end of each meeting we'd all pray.

It was late 1993, and one day when we stood up to pray, my friend's wife began reciting a scripture in which Jesus says, "These signs will accompany those who have believed: in My name they will cast out demons, they will speak with new tongues; they will pick up serpents, and [here's my part] if they drink any deadly *poison*, it will not hurt them" (Mark 16:17–18, NAS).

When I heard that, I immediately became overwhelmed. The Lord was speaking to me, saying, "My Word was working in your life back then." Understand, this is more than twenty years later—the day I drank that poison was the furthest thing from my mind. It was nothing I contemplated or reflected on. It was in the past, a part of my childhood.

I felt as if God was saying to me, "Do you remember all those people who visited you in the hospital?" I started going over it in my head: the friends, relatives, doctors. He said, "I visited you then. Although you didn't see Me, I was with you." I fell to my knees, weeping, realizing God's absolute goodness and understanding the significance and power of His Word. Realizing His love for me, and realizing His Word performed this miracle in my life, was completely overwhelming.

When I finally regained my composure and told everyone about the poison I drank twenty years earlier, and then what happened when the scripture was recited, they joined me in thanking Jesus. To this day I can think about it and weep.

If you aren't sure God is real, ask Him to reveal Himself. If you're honest, I'm confident He'll show Himself to you.

If you know the Lord, continue to believe in Him and stand on His Word. Believe for your health but understand that God is in control. Step back, let Him handle things, and rely upon Him. The Bible says, "In all your ways acknowledge Him, and He shall direct your paths" (Prov. 3:6). The more you do that, the better off you'll be, knowing too that "all things work together for good to those who love God" (Rom. 8:28).

 **Mark Russak** is a dedicated follower of Jesus Christ who is passionate about using technology and the arts to communicate the good news of Jesus Christ. He writes and teaches on the validity of the Scriptures, with an emphasis on providing sound, logical answers to much of society's objections to the Christian faith. Mark is an accomplished voice-over artist, writer, producer, and engineer whose career has been in various forms of multimedia and broadcast television. He is also active in his local church. Mark and his wife live on Long Island, New York, and have two grown sons. For more information, write markr@voiceovermark.com or visit www.voiceovermark.com.

26

The Cowboy Prophet

And He called the twelve to Himself, and
began to send them out two by two....He
commanded them to take nothing for the
journey except a staff—no bag, no bread, no
copper in their money belts....So they went
out and preached that people should repent.

MARK 6:7–8, 12

*M*Y NAME IS Jules Ostrander. I was born in 1952. I'm a cattle
rancher from Nebraska. My family has been in the cattle business since
the 1880s. While I was attending the University of Nebraska, a fellow student invited me to a Bible study on the Book of John to explore who Jesus
was. Through the meeting, the students, and the instruction, I came to
know Jesus as my personal Savior in 1971. I have attended seminary and
done several things for God since then. But then God directed me to
New York City after the World Trade Center towers came down.

After 9/11 I was talking to somebody, and I said, "We have a God
problem in America—not a political problem or a terrorist problem—
we're in trouble with God." The part that startled me was when I said,
"Somebody should be tromping across America warning people to repent."
This rolled out of my mouth, and I said to myself, "That's quite a thought.
There must be a pastor, missionary, or unemployed man who could take
up that task."

Several weeks later I heard a Native American woman share her testimony about how she never did anything for God until she was fifty years
old. I was forty-nine-and-a-half, and I began shaking inside. I knew God

was saying, "You're the man. It's New York City. I didn't tell anyone else to do this. I told you."

That day I told my pastor. Then I told the Lord I would go to New York. I told Him, "If I had an invitation, I would take off today." When I was reading the Bible and praying, I sensed the Lord saying, "You don't need an invitation. Go to New York and talk to anybody who will listen."

I had fifty-six dollars, three quarters of a tank of gasoline, and a prayer. I headed to New York City by faith. I had no invitation; nobody knew I was coming. Nebraska is halfway to California from New York. You can't possibly make it to New York on fifty-six dollars. But I started out, and God began to direct me. I visited several places. I didn't ask anybody for any money. I just did what God had said to do: I told people to repent and that we were in trouble with God.

Several days passed, and I visited various people I knew. They listened and let me stay in their homes and fed me, but nobody gave me any traveling money. After five days I was only four hundred miles from home.

Then I met up with a college friend whom I'd led to the Lord in the seventies, and he gave me one hundred dollars. Later that day, as I was driving, the Lord said, "Stop at this church." So I stopped at a church I'd never been to before and met a man I didn't know. I visited a while with him, and he gave me six dollars. Later that night I visited with a roofing contractor at a restaurant. This was a wealthy man. He owned the restaurant, as well as a construction company. He cleaned out the money from his cash register, wadded it up, and handed it to me.

"That's $500 cash," he said. "If that doesn't get you to New York, call me. I'm good for more." That day, $606 had come in, and about six weeks later, in early December 2001, I arrived in New York.

I knew only one man in New York, a pastor in Smithtown, Long Island. He took me to Ground Zero the next morning. I had never ridden a subway. I'd never been in Manhattan, never been around so many people. Where I live, it's twenty miles to the nearest town and fifty miles to the nearest stoplight.

I started going to the city every day from Long Island, and God miraculously connected me with people—a banker one night, a hairdresser another. People began giving me rides out of the city back to Long

Island. I found out there was a Gideons International meeting at a diner in Smithtown, and I crashed it one morning. They put me at the head of the table and bought my breakfast.

"What's your name, what's your business, when did you come to know Jesus, and do you have a daily quiet time?" the president asked. I guess I passed his test because he said, "Tell us what you're doing in town."

I learned that he knew the banker from the night before and the hairdresser! I thought there were millions of people in New York City! Apparently everybody knows each other! It turned out they all attended the same church in Dix Hills, even though I met them in different places. It was strange.

The Gideons president said, "I'm scheduled to speak on Wednesday night, but you can come speak. I'll give you my time slot." That was the beginning. For more than seven years I've spoken in churches, businessmen's clubs, diners, and on TV. I go to New York for thirty days, come home and tend to the cows and see the children for thirty days, and then go back for thirty days. My wife, Lynette, goes in several times a year, and we've fallen in love with New York. We love people, and God put it on my heart to preach on the love of God—that God loves people, and He loves America. God also wants me to hammer away on sin and corruption.

I get paid for the days I'm on the ranch. The days I'm gone, I don't. My wife doesn't work outside the home. It takes miraculous provision for me to feed my wife and family, and buy plane tickets and such. The Lord has prompted me not to charge when I speak—not even to ask for traveling expenses. If the Lord calls, He pays. We speak in all kinds of places free of charge, so every day is a miracle. Filling up the gas tank is a miracle!

We stay in private homes. God provides the transportation. We have a car that we leave in New York that was bought and paid for by New Yorkers. I've never brought more than fifty dollars with me for my monthlong stays on Long Island. I've never even had to take a cab from the airport. A New Yorker has been there to pick me up every time. God miraculously provides for all of our needs.

We love people from all denominations, as well as people who have never heard about God; we love helping them to have a relationship with Him. You need a firsthand, personal relationship with God too. He loves you!

Jules Ostrander has a deep, God-given love for people that spurs his authentic passion for God's people to hear the voice of the Lord and experience His holy fire and power. Today he and his family live in North Dakota, where they minister to the workers of the Bakken oil fields. Jules continues to visit New York and believe God for spiritual revival in America. For more information, write jostrand52@gmail.com.

27

The Power of the Spirit

For our gospel did not come to you in
word only, but also in power, and in the
Holy Spirit and in much assurance.

1 THESSALONIANS 1:5

*M*Y NAME IS Steven Delopoulos. I was born in Red Bank,
New Jersey, in 1974 to Greek parents. My spiritual background is Greek
Orthodox. My first language was Greek, and my mother played Greek
music in the house when I was growing up. She also prayed in Greek. She
prayed the Lord's Prayer with my sister and me every night. Hearing the
prayer meant a lot to me because I knew it represented this connection
with God. As she prayed, I'd close my eyes and really want to be touched
by God.

As I grew up, I got involved in the arts. I'm a musician, and I attended
an acting college and did lots of theater. Acting helped me learn to relax.
In prayer you need to relax and expect to be touched by God's presence.

During college, I experimented with drugs. I did LSD, which really
changed my way of thinking and looking at life. It freaked me out
because it caused me to lose the innocence and freedom I felt during my
childhood. I felt damaged from the drugs. Then I met Christians, and I
started praying and tried changing my perspective.

When I was eighteen, I was on a boat with my parents going to Greece,
and I remember feeling completely chained, as if I was entangled. I knelt
down, looked up at the stars, and said, "God, if You're real, make Yourself
known and available to me. I'm tired of me." I felt fed up.

For about a year and a half after that God started talking to me through people, literature, the Bible, and church. Then came an amazing experience.

I was on a bus heading home to New Jersey after doing a play in Manhattan. A young woman approached me and said, "The Spirit of God told me to sit next to you. Do you mind?" I was very into the idea of miracles occurring, so I didn't mind. I invited her to sit, and we had a great talk all the way back. She explained that she was a Christian and that amazing miracles were happening in her church. (Looking back, I realize it was a Pentecostal church where people experienced the Holy Spirit.)

Toward the end of our talk I asked if she would pray with me, which she agreed to. We held hands, and I asked who should pray first (I was used to organized prayer). She said we both would pray at once, so we closed our eyes and started whispering prayers. In that innocence, that sudden moment of faith, I opened my eyes and this dimension was gone—I was in a heavenly realm!

I felt a rain of love fall over me. "Wow! I'm in heaven!" I thought. I saw and heard angels. I felt God talking to me. When I opened my eyes, the young woman was shining, glowing! I didn't see a person; I saw an angel. The experience lasted only about twenty seconds, but it felt like it lasted an eternity.

When my mother saw me after I arrived home a short time later, she started crying. She kept crying, saying, "You've changed! You've changed!" When my father saw me, he threw a lamp against the wall—he was so confused and stunned. His son wasn't walking into that house; it was as if the Holy Spirit was walking into that house!

The Holy Spirit had just touched me through what I saw as an angel. I was transformed. I was feeling electrified by the vast love I felt. I was "drunk" from the power of the Holy Spirit (see Acts 2:14–17), and His presence lingered with me. My parents saw it and were freaked out.

That experience at about age eighteen changed my life completely because I lost the fear of death. I realized there was something else after the physical dimension ends. It was real and powerful. I knew God had touched me.

Another experience I had was when my parents were getting divorced.

I was about twenty-two years old. I was sad they were divorcing and feeling really down, so I took my Bible and went to the beach at Sandy Hook, New Jersey. I remember being by the ocean, praying, cursing God, and asking, "Why, God? Why?"

I had a vision. It was like a news flash of what God wanted from me. First I saw a flash of Christ and then I saw a flash of me sitting on a stool, playing guitar, my hand on the audience and God's Spirit going from my hand to the people. This was before I was a musician. Now I happen to play professionally both as a solo artist and with the band Burlap to Cashmere.

That experience also really guided me in the right direction toward what I should be doing in my ministry.

There have been other instances of divine intervention, but those are the most powerful and extreme because they clearly were not coming from my imagination. I can tell when I've had too much coffee and my imagination is flowing. I can definitely differentiate the coffee from having an actual out-of-body experience in the presence of something magnified, big, and grand that's limitless and full of love. The experience on the bus changed my life. To this day I believe if I tap into that power again I could move mountains and heal people the way Christ taught us.

If you're not sure God exists, and you are seeking Him, my advice is not to force it. I'm a big believer in the process of grace. If you leave God notes and you let God know you're searching, God will let you know how it's done.

In the Bible Paul talks about working out your salvation "with fear and trembling" (Phil. 2:12). Your seeking never ends. You're always seeking out your salvation. The process of being in grace, the process of being alive and being human—the power and paradox of that—is difficult. My advice would be, a little at a time: little steps at a time, little realizations at a time. You can't dive into the great "I Am" (Exod. 3:14) without the process.

You can have a real, alive, energetic, intuitive relationship with God—it's free, it's yours, and you don't have to answer to anyone else for it. That's why we're here. We're born to experience that joy of knowing Him.

 **Steven Delopoulos** is a soulful story-teller, a graceful and gritty singer, with guitar chops to boot, whose hard-won and hopeful songs transport listeners from the dream-filled American road to the colorful streets of Greece. In addition to a successful career as a solo artist he is also lead vocalist, songwriter, and guitarist for the band Burlap to Cashmere. For more information, visit www.facebook.com/stevendelopoulos or www.burlaptocashmere.com.

28

God Loves Bikers

Preserve my life, for I am holy;
You are my God;
Save Your servant who trusts in You!

PSALM 86:2

MY NAME IS Joe Pinto. I was born in Queens, New York, in 1961, and I still live in New York. I'm a professional mechanic by trade, with more than twenty years' experience. I trained in the military and have worked on airplanes, boats, cars, and motorcycles. I want to share a story of God's hand of protection over my life. This was a big wake-up call for me that God is real.

During the summer of 2003, I was having problems with my motorcycle. It broke down, and I stored it in the garage while I rode my son's bike. I'd taken the axle nut off my bike and put it on my son's bike because his nut was missing; it was stripped and no good and needed to be replaced. So I used the one from my bike for the time being.

I finally repaired my bike. It was a Friday morning when I started it up, went to the gas station, and filled it up. I rode to work that day then rode home. Work was in Huntington, New York, thirty-seven miles from my house. I rode there and back running at highway speed, which for me is seventy-five miles per hour or more. This is especially true in the mornings, riding in the carpool lane. I just go!

The next day, Saturday, my daughter and I got on my bike and drove from where we live in Coram to Freeport to catch a party boat—and we were late. I rode with her on the back of the bike at around ninety miles per hour—all the way to Freeport—about forty-five miles. We went fishing and had a great day. We got back on the bike and rode home. It was a normal ride, a nice leisurely ride home for another forty-five miles.

The next day I was leaving for Pennsylvania for a week's vacation. On Sunday morning I got on my bike, started it, left the driveway, and went to the gas station about a mile away and put gas in the bike. I made a left turn out of the gas station, and the bike started to shake. "Whoa! This isn't right," I thought. I turned the wheel again, and the bike shook noticeably and started fishtailing.

I pulled the bike over, and when I looked underneath, I knew immediately what I had done. There was no nut holding the axle in place on the back wheel! I had forgotten to replace it when I stopped riding my son's bike! Because there was no nut, the axle had moved about two inches out from where it should've been. I started the bike and gingerly drove home. I took the nut off the other bike, put it back on mine, made the adjustment, tightened it up, and then was able to drive to Pennsylvania.

I believe it was God's hand that held the wheel on. I'd driven about one hundred seventy-five miles, all at high speeds (it was all highway riding), with no nut holding the axle in place! I believe God had His hand on the axle all that time.

But on Sunday morning He showed me He was letting go and said, "Hey, I'm not holding it anymore. It's time to remember that you left this thing off." That was clear evidence to me that God is real. Think about it: There's no nut on the other end holding it all together. The axle's just a shaft. You have a wheel spinning, and without a nut holding it on the shaft it's just going to walk out.

I'm a professional mechanic and have been working on bikes for many, many years. Under normal circumstances it shouldn't have lasted more than about ten miles before coming out, especially at highway speeds. If that wheel had come off or seized up while we were riding at those speeds, either my daughter, I, or both of us could have been killed.

This is a major testimony to the Lord's protection over our lives, and I'm so grateful for His mercy toward us. It truly was a divine intervention!

Joe Pinto is an active member of his congregation at City on a Hill Community Church in Middle Island, New York, where he serves as head of grounds and maintenance, head usher, and enjoys singing for the annual Easter cantata. Joe lives with his wife and children on Long Island, New York. For more information, write trucks38@aol.com.

29

Breaking Through the Darkness

Those who are wise shall shine like
the brightness of the firmament, and
those who turn many to righteousness
like the stars forever and ever.

DANIEL 12:3

*M*Y NAME IS Joanna Swanson. I was born in Arizona in 1981. My parents divorced when I was one year old, and a stepfather entered the scene when I was about three. Life wasn't great when I was little. I suffered much abuse as a child—physical, sexual, emotional, and even satanic ritual abuse. I didn't have your typical American upbringing. My stepfather was involved in witchcraft, and I led a double life. I attended school during the day, trying to act like a normal child and not talking about the occultism and abuse happening behind the scenes.

Many professionals are involved in the satanic church: lawyers, doctors, teachers, and police. It's a secret society; members don't want their identities exposed. I remember as a child being taken to rituals—often in a warehouse, a house, or sometimes a cave. The rituals were all different but had the same feel. There would be a fire or candles, and the members would do séances and blood covenants. And there was always sacrifice involved, whether animal or human. It was horrible and traumatizing, and instilled such fear in me. Although this was part of my "normal" life, I understood that it was wrong and evil.

Mom worked continually. She was in an abusive relationship, so her escape was work. She knew we were around people who were involved in wicked things, but I don't believe she knew the extent of it until years later when we were free from my stepfather and that life.

Once you belong to a coven, the witches own you and are responsible for training and minding you. They taught me through séances and rituals how to see into the spirit world, and about astral projection—out-of-body experiences. I learned how I could make my spirit and soul leave my body.

The first time it happened, I was in an abandoned house they used for rituals. I was sitting in the center of an engraved pentagram with lit candles on the points of the star. My body was on the floor, but I was seeing everything from the ceiling. I was very aware that I wasn't in my body. I had no fear and felt empowered, which is why people like to do this; they have a sense of control. You don't really have control, but you think so at the time. Ultimately you're being influenced by demons and fallen angels.

When you're out of your body, the normal laws of physics don't apply; you're not stuck in your body in a physical sense. You actually can see the spirit realm—everything as it actually is. I was involved in this until about age sixteen. As you age and mature in this kind of thing, you feel like you're getting more power, but you're actually acquiring more bondage.

This is the thing I have to explain: There are laws of darkness and laws of righteousness. I knew nothing of the laws of righteousness then. I only knew about the laws of darkness because a witch was mentoring me. The more you taint God's Word and practice lawlessness and disobedience, the more power you'll have through demonic spirits. It's the first commandment in the Black Bible: "Do What Thou Wilt."

There's no law or authority for you. You do what you want. You're taught that the more disobedient and rebellious against authority you are, the more power you'll receive. But it's a lie! You're actually receiving evil spirits. Later in life you realize they control you and actually possess you. This was my life for years.

Mom had some Christian friends who advised her to escape from my stepfather. They didn't know the extent of the abuse at home, but they knew our lives were in danger. One night I was staying at my friend's house, and Mom picked me up with a U-Haul and said, "Say good-bye. We're leaving."

I was twelve and had two teenage sisters. We drove straight through to

Minnesota, and with the help of a Christian family, settled in Rochester. Mom got help through family counseling and was trying to get her life back together. She always had a strong heart and was a woman of faith. She did the best she could with what she knew. I knew that in her heart she wanted what was best for her children. I didn't receive the healing I needed from counseling, so I moved out of Mom's house at age fifteen.

Life went on, and by seventeen I was depressed, addicted to drugs and alcohol, and was also selling drugs. I still dabbled in witchcraft, but it wasn't a huge part of my life anymore, since I didn't have a coven and had left my stepfather and those things behind. I was still able to see into the spirit realm, however. For the most part I could ignore it and go on doing my everyday tasks without really noticing demonic forces or the spirit realm. But at any moment I could look and see what was happening. Most of the time I tried to ignore what I was seeing.

Then I had a terrifying experience I couldn't ignore, and it led me to seek God. One night I was with my fiancé. It was our daily activity to do drugs, whether pot, meth, acid, or alcohol—that was our normal life. We'd taken some acid, when my fiancé's poodle abruptly became agitated and began barking frantically.

We were sitting on the bed when I suddenly noticed demons were filling the room. There were always demons present, but not like the hordes that were coming in this night. They began taunting me, saying things such as, "We have you" and "We're taking you." I had a feeling I was going to die that night. I looked around the room, and the walls started turning to blood, flames of fire started shooting out of the floor, and I could see down below. It was black, and all I could hear was shrieking screams from souls who were in darkness.

There really are no words to describe what I experienced. It was so horrific that my heart started beating out of my chest from hearing the screams. It was horrible! I feared I'd have a heart attack while listening to the screams. All I could see was complete black, total darkness—a feeling of being utterly alone. On earth we don't have that feeling because we're surrounded with people—family, parents—there's always somebody. Even if you feel lonely, it doesn't compare to what I felt in that atmosphere. It was the most isolating feeling you could imagine! In that moment I had a sense of the reality of absolute darkness and aloneness that hell is—such indescribable suffering.

Then suddenly this experience ended, and both my fiancé and I were completely sober. He experienced it too, and we talked about it the next day. I knew in my heart I was perishing and headed for hell. I needed a Savior and I needed help. I knew hell was real, and I didn't want to go there. What I experienced was so gripping that I couldn't get it off my mind. I didn't know whom to talk to or what to do.

My sister, whom I hadn't spoken with in years, "happened" to call me that week and invited me to hang out. She took me to a church where an evangelist was speaking. I have no idea what he spoke on because I was so nervous—I was very uncomfortable being there. I didn't know my sister was already a born-again believer and had been praying for me. The evangelist called me out of the crowd and said God wanted to speak to me. I stood there, slightly curious. Because of my background I knew how tarot cards, fortune-tellers, and mediums worked. There are certain things I knew you could and couldn't do, so I was skeptical.

The man said, "Joanna, God knows you and the number of hairs on your head. He wants me to tell you these five things..." And when he said "five," he had my attention. From the time I was little I'd been raped and much had been taken from me. I decided at a young age there would be five things nobody would be able to take from me. I'd never speak or write them; they would be mine alone to know. They would be ways I'd live—not morals per se, but values in my heart that nobody would ever know about. I held on to those five things. They gave me some form of worth because they couldn't be stolen from me.

So when he said, "five things," my heart stopped and I listened. This man proceeded to list my five secret values—in order. Nobody could have known that—no medium, no sorcerer, no tarot card reader—nobody. I never spoke them or wrote them. There's no way anyone—except God—could have known them.

There was no way I could deny God was real and that He was speaking through this man. I was shocked. I couldn't believe what I was hearing. The man continued, "Joanna, God has a new life for you. If you'll give Him your heart and surrender your life to Him, He'll give you a new life."

I went home that night, got on my knees, and said, "God, I know You're real, and I need Your help. I need You to intervene in my life." I was involved in drugs and all sorts of things, and I didn't know what to do. I felt like my whole life was interrupted.

I ended up moving out of my apartment and living with my sister. She started mentoring me. She said, "There's only one rule in my house: I'm going to pray with you, and we're going to read one chapter from the Bible every day—that's it. You're a big girl, and you can do what you want."

Her praying and reading the Scriptures with me every morning, one chapter every day, literally brought me to spiritual health. God began renewing my mind and speaking to me powerfully through His Word. I began to know Jesus Christ in a powerful way through the Holy Spirit.

I had been all messed up. Because of my background I was full of hate, unforgiveness, and bitterness. I couldn't stop swearing, smoking, doing drugs, or dressing immodestly because I was so bound and fearful. But through the Word and the Holy Spirit, God brought healing and restoration. Today I'm renewed and free! It's as if those things in my past never happened.

I'm a speaker, prayer counselor, and model. My sister and I founded Embracing Miracles Ministries after finding peace and hope in Christ. God sends me many people who have come out of abuse of all kinds. I can empathize with them and know how to help them because I've lived through it and know the power of the gospel to set people free. Jesus is real. You might be disappointed with church, but when you seek Jesus, you'll find Him. Jesus is the Savior, and He's the only One who can restore and save you!

Joanna Swanson is a speaker, prayer counselor, model, and doula. She is also the president of Embracing Miracles Ministries, for which she travels extensively, ministering the gospel. She lives in Texas with her husband and children. For more information, write Joanna.lwa@gmail.com.

30

Pick Up Your Mat and Walk

He [Jesus] said to the [paralytic], "I
tell you, get up, take your mat and go
home." He got up, took his mat and
walked out in full view of them all.

MARK 2:10–12, NIV

MY NAME IS Dani Johnson. I'm a professional speaker,
author, and business and life coach. I hope my testimony encourages you
to know that God is real, He loves you, and no matter what your background, you can succeed in life.

I was born in California in 1969 to drug-addicted parents who fought
often. My stepfather was six feet, ten inches tall and weighed three hundred sixty pounds. He was an absolute giant, especially to three little
girls—my two sisters and me. My parents did lots of drugs: cocaine, marijuana, reds, whites, uppers, downers. And as I got older, I suffered physical, verbal, and sexual abuse. I was sexually violated by a relative for four
years until I moved away from home at age sixteen. I had a violent, horrific childhood.

My stepfather was an atheist, and my mother an agnostic. I'd given
my life to Jesus at a school chapel service at age thirteen. I then walked
away from God at eighteen due to some painful experiences I had with
the church I was attending. I said, "God, if I have to be like Your people,
I want nothing to do with You."

I started in business at nineteen and plunged into the metaphysical
world of crystals, psychics, tarot cards, and more. My first six months
in business I totally failed. The next six months, after finding a mentor,
I had huge success. Then I married a guy after knowing him only seven

days. My husband drained my bank account, maxed out my credit cards, embezzled my business, and left me with a $35,000 debt and $2.03 to my name. I lost *everything*. I wasn't walking with God; I was following false gods and didn't realize it. I'd been so hurt by the church that I was scared to even *talk* to God.

I was homeless, living on a beach, terrified of being raped and of having the few things I actually owned stolen. I was three thousand miles away from anything familiar. My husband had moved me to Hawaii, which I hated—I was a cowgirl, not a beach bum. I was confused, distraught, suicidal, and desperate. I was doing everything I said I'd never do: drugs, drinking, working at a bar, and hanging out with people who were cheating on their spouses and partying constantly. It blows my mind when I think about it, but because I was in such a deep depression and had lost my first love (God), I did the unthinkable: cocaine.

On Christmas Eve I was at a party in the bar where I worked, and the bartender invited me to her car. I was drunk and high on marijuana; no part of my right mind was functioning. The bartender and I were sitting in her Volkswagen Bug, and she opened the glove compartment. There was some white powder, a razor, and a straw. That was the one thing I said I'd *never* do. I took a *vow* that I'd never do cocaine because cocaine destroyed our family.

But I snorted a line, returned to the party, and just danced. I don't remember where or with whom I slept that night, nor where I awoke. I was "goners." The next day there was a beach party at the same bar, and I can't remember how I got there. I went from person to person asking for more cocaine, saying, "Where do I get more of that stuff? Erin (not her real name) gave me a line. Where do I get more?" They looked at me like I was crazy.

Erin said, "Nobody else at the bar does that stuff! Are you nuts?"

"I must get more," I said. "I'll do anything for it. How much is it, and how do I get a whole lot of it?" I would have sold my body for cocaine if it had been available. It *gripped* me. It took hold of me like nothing ever had. I would have given anything for another line.

Frustrated that I couldn't find more cocaine, I went for a swim in the ocean. I dove beneath a wave and upon coming out of the water, I heard a voice. The voice said, "Pick up your mat and walk." Instantly I lost the desire for cocaine. The frustration and pain, the thing that made me unable to think straight, left *instantaneously*. I turned, walked to my beach mat, rolled it up, and left.

While driving to the beach I had been living on, there was a conversation going on in my head. One side, I believe, was the devil; the other, I believe, was God.

One voice said, "You're a loser and a failure. Look at you—you did cocaine, you've been sleeping around. You're exactly like your parents. Your husband didn't love you. Your father didn't love you. You're a worthless piece of trash."

The other voice said, "This isn't the life I intended for you. It's time to step up, get away from these people, and do what you know you can do. You know better than to live this way."

I knew God had spoken to me. The next day I started a business using the trunk of my car and a payphone booth. I had no product or service. All I had were some skills I'd worked hard developing the year before that I'd abandoned when my business was embezzled.

I started applying those skills. I called a company to try and license a product that I'd purchased and had sitting in my car. I licensed it, generated $2,000 the first ten hours and $6,500 the next month. I quit my waitressing job, made $125,000 that year, and made my first million dollars by the end of my second year—all by age twenty-three.

I eventually began walking with Christ again, but I learned the gospel through business in the marketplace, not in the church. I've since become a multimillionaire, having coached many others along the way. I have more than three hundred thousand clients worldwide and have been featured on many media outlets, such as Fox News and ABC's *Secret Millionaire*. The principles I teach are biblically based, and we see many people get saved and healed at my secular business seminars.

God has a plan for you, and it isn't for you to be impoverished, unhappy, depressed, or even mediocre. He calls His people to something far greater. If you want God to be for you instead of against you, call upon Him through the name Jesus Christ, the name that's above every name. What He's done in my life, He can do in yours. It's not about a church or religion. It's about the Creator of heaven and earth directing you to greatness.

Dani Johnson is a former cocktail waitress who was broke and homeless before, in two short years, she became a millionaire after following God's vision for her life. Her passion is to show people how to attain great success in every area of their lives without sacrificing their family, their fun, or their health. As president and cofounder of Call to Freedom International and cofounder of King's Ransom Foundation, a nonprofit serving people in need worldwide, Dani is helping thousands to live victorious, successful lives. For more information, visit www.danijohnson.com.

31

Brooklyn Born, Israel Bound!

That I may know Him and the
power of His resurrection, and the
fellowship of His sufferings.

PHILIPPIANS 3:10

*Dedicated to my beloved children
Richie and Linda*

MY NAME IS Liz Alberti. I was born in Brooklyn, New York, in 1944. At age twelve I started questioning life. Being raised Catholic, I wanted to become a nun and connect with the spiritual part of life. My parents didn't take that idea seriously and figured I'd get over it, which I did, but I knew there was more to life than I was experiencing. I started searching in spiritual ways, not knowing G-d or Jesus. I married at nineteen and had two children by twenty-one.

In 1971 my husband was leaving, and it was devastating. I had two children and no money. One day we went to my brother-in-law's house on Long Island. My sister-in-law, Joan (who was Jewish), asked to pray for me. She prayed, but I didn't pray. I just called on Jesus.

Suddenly I left the earth and went into another dimension with Him. I heard Joan saying something, which I later learned was praying in tongues. As she prayed alongside me, I started shaking violently. I was in the grip of something so powerful and loving; my body couldn't sustain itself in this overwhelming presence of pure love. On April 17, 1971, I met Jesus and fell madly in love with Him.

Joan found a good congregation in Brooklyn for me to attend. They focused on understanding Israel and the Jews. Meanwhile my husband went away, eventually divorcing me, which was very difficult. One night, while reading the Bible and telling Jesus how much I loved Him, I began speaking in tongues. A language I didn't understand was coming out of my mouth! It scared me. I thought, "I'm doing what Joan does! I'm weird, but this is bizarre!" I didn't understand that this was a gift of the Holy Spirit.

Jesus then clearly said, "Pray for Judah's return."

Perplexed, I asked, "Who's Judah? Where does he live?"

"You will minister to My people," He said, "but you must first *become* My people. You'll be isolated and misunderstood, but I will train you."

And He did. The Lord started training me to understand His heart for His people as a Gentile—a non-Jew. He gave me a heart for the Jews and Israel that today, more than thirty-five years later, is as ferocious as it was then. I devoured the Bible and read almost nothing else.

I was the church superintendent for eight years. I taught Sunday school, my daughter taught kindergarten, and the church had a Jewish nucleus. We celebrated Passover and taught what Passover meant, and how it tied into Jesus (*Yeshua* in Hebrew), the Passover (*Pasach*) Lamb.

In 1982 I attended Bible school where G-d was developing me into an intercessor, someone who "intercedes" in prayer for people or situations. After graduating, I took a secretarial job in New Jersey. While furnishing my new apartment, the Lord said, "You won't be here long. Only get the necessities."

"Where am I going, Lord?"

"Just get what you need," He said. I bought a couch and a bed. Everything else, people gave me.

In the summer of 1983, while reading the Bible, I experienced a phenomenon called *rhema*. It's when G-d's Word comes off the page and is meant just for you. It's no longer *logos* (the written word); it's *rhema* (the spoken word). The Lord clearly said, "Get ready. You're going to Israel." I'd always wanted to go to Israel. I'd been praying to go for years.

G-d gave me scriptures about living in the land of Israel. I wrote them in my journal, then danced, cried, and laughed for joy. I started preparing. I got my passport and sold my things. I didn't know what was happening—I only knew I was going to Israel. My family thought I was crazy.

Then a friend introduced me to an Israeli man who "happened" to need a secretary. I said, "Hi. I'm Liz Alberti. The Lord is calling me to Israel."

"Liz, if G-d is calling you, you'll make it," he said. "If He's not, Israel's a tough place to be, spiritually speaking. Let's pray that if G-d wants you there He'll open the doors for you, but if not, He'll close them." We prayed, then he said, "Send me your résumé and how you became a believer."

I sent him the information and put my situation in G-d's hands. His office contacted me, saying they wanted me immediately. Two months later I was in Israel! G-d was right when He said I wouldn't be in New Jersey long; I lived there only four months.

In Israel my name became *Elisheva*, meaning, "vowed to G-d" in Hebrew. I studied Hebrew in an *ulpan*, a school for learning the language. I had a B visa, which allows you to stay ninety days. If you're attending school, they aren't likely to bother you, but they don't like Gentiles staying in Israel. They're very leery of non-Jews. They don't want to hear about Jesus, and as a Gentile I had no rights. If they caught me speaking about Jesus, I could be deported.

I prayed about this and the Lord said, "Although it will be rough staying in Israel as a Gentile, I will take care of you." And He did. Through many instances of divine intervention, I stayed *nine years*, living by faith the whole time, with no income. Yet I had money for plane tickets to visit my family and money to send when there were birthdays. G-d always provided enough for food, rent, whatever I needed.

I lived six years with an Orthodox woman from Russia who taught me how to keep kosher and live as a Jew. She loved me, and I was able to tell her about Jesus. We attended Synagogue together every Friday, and lit Shabbat candles.

My time in Israel was gloriously supernatural. I saw angels manifest, and I experienced a miraculous recovery from a stroke and paralysis—with no medical treatment, just prayer and G-d's Word. I even volunteered for six months in the Israeli army during the Gulf War.

Then after nine years G-d closed the door. I went to renew my visa, and the official asked, "Why are you here? How are you living?" She was very suspicious. I always stayed within the law, never working for money. I stayed with friends, cleaned their houses and watched their children, and was given room and board. She told me I had to leave immediately.

I was devastated but returned to America, eventually readjusting to life here. G-d continues to move in my life today. How wonderful these past thirty-five-plus years have been, walking with Jesus!

Liz Alberti (pictured here with two fellow members of the Israeli army, early 1990s) is retired from the workforce but still ministers the gospel, counsels people in the Lord's ways, and educates people about Israel. She lives on Long Island, New York. For more information, write elizabethelishevaliz@yahoo.com.

32

From Communism to Christ

Have mercy upon me, O God, according
to your lovingkindness; according to
the multitude of your tender mercies,
blot out my transgressions.

PSALM 51:1

Y NAME IS Maria Baron. I was born in Hungary in 1935.
I had a very religious Orthodox grandmother, and I attended church
until the seventh grade. The priest trusted me with telling stories from
the Old Testament to the other kids in my class. I tried to observe all the
religious rituals, such as fasts and holidays, from my youth.

In 1944 when the Russians invaded Hungary, religion was prohibited
and everyone had to be an atheist. This had a profound effect on our
society and on my family. Everyone was afraid of losing their jobs, and
they all did what the government requested. My religious grandmother
was the only one left in our family who had a Bible. She prayed continually at the back of the house where no one could see her. Her youngest
son, who took care of her until she died, didn't bury her religiously. She
had a state funeral, with a band playing the country's anthem and other
nationalistic songs.

I grew up and became a schoolteacher. As a teacher I had to do a lot
of ungodly things, such as chasing kids away from church and forbid-
ding topics that had to do with God in the classroom (or even outside the
school), as any talk of God was considered propaganda. Mentioning the
word *God* was punishable, and anyone heard saying it would be ridiculed
and reported to supervisors at work. If a child was caught attending

church, it was the schoolteacher's job to condemn the child's parents for polluting the child's mind. It was an ongoing job.

I became an outstanding atheist. At each public event I was the first to participate and make public speeches praising the government and the Communist Party for the wonderful life they'd given us. I would make my speeches personable (especially at funerals), and people really enjoyed them. People started writing me requesting me to give speeches about their deceased loved ones. I don't think they cared that all the praises were always given to the government and to the Communist Party, but never to God.

Even though outwardly I was an atheist and a Communist, deep down I knew God was there. I felt God's presence often. Whenever I had a problem and needed His help, I would ask God to intervene. He never hesitated. My requests were always answered.

In 1987 a dramatic event occurred in my life that caused me to truly seek God and return to Him. I developed a large cyst inside my leg muscle, and the doctors diagnosed it as an incurable form of cancer. I had two unsuccessful surgeries attempting to remove it, but the cancer remained.

The doctors' prognosis was not good when I went in for the third surgery. They said that even if they were able to remove the cyst, the best-case scenario I could expect would be that I would live seven years. They said less than 1 percent of people live seven years after being diagnosed with this type of cancer.

As I was waiting in the hospital before going in for my third surgery, I saw another woman in the waiting area reading a Bible. I was at a loss and very sad, and I asked her what I should pray before my surgery. She told me to sincerely pray Psalm 51 (which deals with forgiveness) and showed it to me:

"Have mercy upon me, O God, according to Your lovingkindness; according to the multitude of Your tender mercies, blot out my transgressions. Wash me thoroughly from my iniquity, and cleanse me from my sin. For I acknowledge my transgressions, and my sin *is* always before me. Against You, You only, have I sinned, and done *this* evil in Your sight" (Ps. 51:1–4).

As I looked back on my life, with all that I did in chasing people away from God, I knew I was a sinner. I sincerely prayed and asked God to forgive me. In fact, I committed my life to Him and asked for at least seven more years to live in exchange for my service to Him. Immediately, I felt like my prayer was answered, and I knew that I would be OK. I felt God's peace and presence.

I went in for the third surgery, and the doctors said it was a success. They still didn't expect me to live more than seven years. They said this cancer always returns. Well, that was more than twenty-five years ago, and I'm still here! I asked for seven years, but God has already given me three times seven! God healed me, and I am so thankful. He is faithful!

I think God reached out to me in many different ways during my life, but it was only my sickness and desire to be around and see my children and grandchildren grow up that brought me back to God. It took cancer entering my body for me to make another dramatic change as well. After the third surgery, when I knew that God had healed me, I had to leave my job to be with God. I did it without hesitation. There was no way I could be with God if I continued teaching in school. I had my degrees, awards, position, and respect at work; and I dropped it all in one day. How could I not, after all He'd done for me? I then started attending church.

I started praying for my husband, who also had to be a Communist Party member to keep his job. He ran state-owned factories and was in charge of packaging and shipping food to other parts of the country. His job was very stressful. He had two heart attacks and had to go on disability.

My husband eventually found a Baptist church through the invitation of a Christian neighbor and became born again. He was baptized ten years after I quit my job. He had such peace and joy in his life up until he got cancer and died in 2003. My daughter, who had been raised as an atheist, had a vision on the day of his funeral, and Christ spoke to her. She became born again and was baptized within a year after her father died.

I am so happy to still be alive and to be able to share my testimony of God's faithfulness in my life. If you are struggling with doubt about God,

I want to encourage you to ask God if He is real, and the answer will be given to you. Follow His will, and you'll be forgiven. God bless you.

Maria Baron is currently living in New York City with her daughter, Libby Baron, while she expectantly awaits her US citizenship. She can be contacted through her daughter at libarvi@gmail.com.

33

The "Paro-dude"

Now to Him who is able to do exceedingly
abundantly above all that we ask or
think, according to the power that works
in us, to Him be glory in the church
by Christ Jesus to all generations.

EPHESIANS 3:20–21

*M*Y NAME IS J. Jackson. I'm lead singer and lyricist for ApologetiX (that Christian parody band). I was born in 1964 and raised Catholic in Pittsburgh, Pennsylvania. I was religious growing up but wasn't satisfied in my relationship with God. I tried to make myself good enough for God, hoping my good deeds would outweigh my bad deeds. I thirsted for something more.

During college, that thirst drove me to search for God through philosophy and science, which left me empty and didn't answer my questions. I also tried reading the Bible but didn't understand it. Frustrated, I quit trying to connect with God, gradually shifting from being religious to hedonistic, trying to always have fun. This also left me empty. One night in 1988 I finally came to the end of myself. I poured out my heart to the Lord in an empty church. I asked Him to guide me and perform a miracle in my life. Things began changing—I was saved.

During the following months, God answered many prayers. I picked up the Bible again. This time it came alive and was like a different book! I read it front to back—Genesis to Revelation. I read it again, then again, and have never stopped. It gets better every time I read it.

Before I got saved, I loved music and was in several bands. Music was like a god to me. That fact disturbed me. So I gave away most of my huge music collection. Meanwhile God changed my heart. I'd always wanted to be a rock star, but I didn't anymore. I just wanted to learn about Jesus and be the best disciple I could be. I immersed myself in the Bible and abandoned all my aspirations for music.

Here's the divine intervention—how God led me back into music. I have a talented guitarist friend who's into rock 'n' roll. We were driving together one day; I'd been born-again about six months at this time.

He said to me, "You may be doing this 'born-again Christian' thing, but you can't abandon rock and roll. It's in your blood."

"No, it's not," I replied. "I'm a new person. God's changed me."

"Well, maybe God can use that and you can do Christian rock and roll," he said.

I just said, "I'm happy as I am."

I dropped him off and started talking to God. I said, "Lord, if You want to do something with music in my life, that would be great. You know I love music, but I'm happy as I am." I made another specific request, praying, "Lord, I read in the Bible about people having the gift of prophecy. I've met people who say they've had prophets give them messages. If You'd like to have that happen to me, that would be really cool."

The next day I stopped into a Burger King in Pittsburgh. There was a guy standing next to me who suddenly said, "You're a Christian, aren't you?"

I wasn't wearing a cross or anything that would identify me as a Christian. I said, "Yeah."

"I can tell," he said. "I see the Holy Spirit all over you. I'm a prophet." He invited me to sit with him, and I did. He started talking, and I listened, but with some suspicion. I wasn't even thinking about what I'd prayed the day before. Then he said something that struck me. In the Bible Paul says if a true prophet speaks, the secrets of a man's heart will be revealed (1 Cor. 14:25).

This man knew nothing about me. All I'd said was that I worked for a printing company. In the course of the conversation he said, "The times in your life when it seemed like everything would come together for you, that you were going to be famous and be somebody, it never happened because God knew if that happened without Him, you'd forget about Him."

The man didn't know that the words he'd just spoken had been on my mind the entire time I'd been a Christian. I had been in bands and performed in musicals, and people would say things like, "You're very talented. You're going to be somebody." But nothing like that ever happened.

But after I got saved, I started to think, "Lord, I believe my music career never took off because You knew if it happened without You, I wouldn't have thought I needed You." Now this guy I'd just met was saying the same thing—something I'd never talked with anyone about.

"Are you into music?" he asked.

"Yeah."

"I thought so. You're a singer, aren't you?"

I hadn't thought of myself as a singer, but I'd been one all my life. I had sung in choirs, bands, and plays, but after I got saved I had abandoned that identity.

"God can use that in your life," he said.

What I've just described might sound simple to you, but consider what I had prayed *the very day before*. It was, "Lord, if You want to use me doing something with music and rock and roll, I'd like that." And, "It would be cool to meet a prophet."

I felt that the "chance" meeting was a divine intervention; those prayers were being answered. I went home and wrote my first two Christian songs. I also picked up the guitar again. God helped me figure out the licks to some old rock songs. But I realized I wasn't comfortable singing those old words. I also wished there was a way I could remember Bible verses. I'd been writing parodies all my life. So I started writing parodies to teach myself both the Bible and the guitar simultaneously. Eventually I started playing them at a Bible study I attended.

I met Karl Messner there. He asked if we could get together and jam. We did and eventually acquired more musicians. We spent two years playing in friends' basements, and at Bible studies and parties.

In 1992 a friend encouraged us to play at a Christian coffeehouse. We chose ApologetiX as our band name for that first show. We didn't know if the people would hate or love what we did. Thankfully they loved the parodies. Since then we have taken every opportunity to play, and God gradually built our success. We've played more than fifteen hundred shows and released more than fifteen albums. We do a hundred shows annually, minimum, and I've been in the band full time for more than ten years.

We get good responses from Christians and non-Christians. Strangely, I think we're the only band that's been featured on both Howard Stern's and Billy Graham's radio shows. How many bands can say that? Also, we've played on *The 700 Club* and the *Dr. Demento* radio show. Our audience is very diverse.

If you don't believe in God, I encourage you to investigate—begin seeking Him. If you get serious about God, you'll discover that He's already very serious about you. If you seek Him with all your heart, you'll find Him, guaranteed!

J. Jackson is lead singer and lyricist for ApologetiX: That Christian Parody Band. He started writing parodies as a kid, influenced by a steady diet of *Mad* magazine, Wacky Packages trading cards, novelty records, and comic books. He became a born-again Christian in January 1988, and his newfound interest in the Bible had a profound influence on his parodies. He cofounded the band ApologetiX in 1992, which to date has released more than twenty albums, performed more than fifteen hundred shows, and has a fan club of multiple thousands. J. lives with his wife and children in Pittsburgh, Pennsylvania. For more information, write to j@apologetix.com or visit www.apologetix.com.

34

Our God Is a Living God

But He was wounded for our transgressions,
He was bruised for our iniquities;
The chastisement for our peace was upon
Him, and by His stripes we are healed.

ISAIAH 53:5

Y NAME IS Mathew John. I was born into a Christian family in India in 1970. At a young age I started working in Abu Dhabi, United Arab Emirates (UAE). In 1991 I married, and God blessed us with a son in 1995.

Although my life was a very happy one, I often suffered from fever and headaches. I had many headaches growing up. I visited many doctors for this condition, but none could find the problem. I was given only pain medication. In November 1998 I got such a severe headache that I went to the hospital. I was given many tests, including an MRI, and eventually they found a tumor inside my pituitary gland and brain.

Unfortunately, biopsies revealed that the tumor was cancerous. They determined that this tumor probably started growing when I was about eleven years old. Suddenly, this unimaginable situation had entered my life. The medical report indicated that I could die within two weeks! My wife and I, along with our community, started praying.

After being hospitalized several days in the UAE, I returned to India and was admitted into a hospital there. The Indian doctors performed more MRIs and scans of my head. The tumor measured roughly six centimeters. They said it had burst inside my brain and was embedded very deep. Initially they said they couldn't do anything for me, but eventually they decided to operate.

During that time, much of it spent in bed, I prayed and begged, "Lord, if You give me another chance at life, I will serve You." God's Word encouraged me, especially Jeremiah 32:27, "Behold, I am the LORD, the God of all flesh. Is there anything too hard for Me?"

On December 1, 1998, I had the surgery. The nine-hour operation was a partial success—of the six-centimeter tumor, the doctors were able to remove a two-centimeter piece. They had to leave the rest because it was so deep in my brain. The tumor had grown through veins and under my eyes. By that time I'd lost my vision but not my faith.

My left eye was 99 percent blind. I continued praying. They biopsied the tumor pieces, and this time, miraculously, the results came back benign—noncancerous! After surgery I had radiation treatment for almost thirty days, which was very hard.

I survived the radiation, and in February 1999, I returned to Abu Dhabi and resumed working at the Sumitomo Corporation, where I'd been for twelve years. I prayed, "Lord, give me six months. After six months I'll serve You for the rest of my life. Whatever You give me to do for You, I will do."

But after the six months were over, I started praying, "Lord, I need financial support to do ministry. I will make some money, then I'll go into ministry." Again, I wanted to delay fulfilling my promise.

On August 3, 1999, God revealed to me, "If you will not fulfill your promise to Me, I will touch you again." I was so scared I resigned my job. I didn't know what to do. I didn't know how to preach. I knew nothing about ministry.

He then said to me, "I am going to send you to the West to study My Word." Normally, to come to America, you must go through lots of red tape and follow certain procedures. In August 1999, however, God did an amazing miracle by opening the doors for me in wonderful ways, just as He said He would. Upon going to the American consulate, I was given a visa (without being asked any questions!) to go to the United States and study at Rhode Island Zion Bible Institute!

When I went to the Abu Dhabi airport to leave for America, God performed another miracle. After I finished at the immigration counter, the power of God came over me and my vision was restored! My left eye had been 99 percent blind, and all that time I was seeing only with my right eye. My left eye was healed that day, and I was able to come to America seeing normally.

Shortly after arriving, I got an MRI at Staten Island University Hospital in New York. The neurosurgeons said, "You should be admitted immediately because there is a four-centimeter tumor in your head." But I believed that God had healed me from the cancer. Although the tumor was still there, I didn't pursue further treatment. I went on to study at Rhode Island Zion Bible Institute, believing I was healed.

One morning in October 2001 I woke up and noticed blood and chunks of tissue coming out of my nose. This scared me. My wife encouraged me and started praying. Because I didn't have medical insurance, I didn't go to the hospital. We just prayed. After eight days the bleeding and tissue discharge stopped, and finally just a clear liquid was coming out my nose. We believe God had performed a miracle and that the tumor had come out through my nose.

I later moved to Seattle, Washington, and studied at Seattle Bible College. On June 2, 2006, I graduated with a bachelor's degree in theology. Early on Monday morning, June 19, I lost my memory and became unconscious. My wife called 911, and I was rushed to the hospital and admitted. The doctors looked at my old MRIs and medical history and, thank God, diagnosed me within two hours. I had meningitis. It was very serious; I was in critical condition and spent almost ten days on a ventilator, unconscious.

When I awoke, I didn't recognize my family. The doctors had also found something interesting in my scans: a hole beneath my brain. Apparently the liquid that came out of my nose after the bleeding episode in 2001 was cerebral fluid. According to medical science, when cerebral fluid leaks, brain function normally will be affected within one week. Mine was not.

The doctors who reviewed my old scans and reports, upon looking at the new ones, asked, "Where is that four-centimeter tumor?" It wasn't visible in the new scans! When my family told them the tumor had come out through my nose, they didn't believe it. They laughed.

After ten days I started recognizing people again. The doctors found that unbelievable. They never expected I would return to normal after the meningitis.

God had given me another miracle! He healed me from the cancer, and I believe He made that small hole underneath my brain so He could remove the tumor through my nose.

I want to encourage you to believe God's Word. I put my faith in God's Word, and God did wonderful things in my life. Praise the Lord!

Mathew John continues to travel and minister the gospel, both in the United States and India. He lives with his wife and son in Texas. For more information, write 4ulord@gmail.com. To view medical documentation, see Appendix.

35

The Pastor and the Close Call

My sheep hear My voice, and I know
them, and they follow Me.

JOHN 10:27

*M*Y NAME IS Richard Jones. I was born in 1956 in Columbia, South Carolina. My father was in the military, and we traveled around some when I was young, but I basically grew up there. My parents became alcoholics due to some painful experiences they went through, so I grew up in that situation.

At age eight I was baptized in the Catholic Church. My dad had gotten sick and thought he was going to die, so he got baptized, and my parents wanted me to be baptized too. Being baptized caused me to realize that Christ was to be there for me, and I wanted to live for Him.

Shortly thereafter my father got drunk at home, fell, and hit his head. That was a scary thing for a little boy to experience, so I went to the park across from our home and started talking to God—yelling at Him, actually. I questioned why I had to live with this family of alcoholics, why I had to go through those things, and how it wasn't fair or right.

As I bared my soul to Him, I felt Him come to me and kind of wipe my tears away. Then He spoke to me, saying it would be OK, that He was still in charge, that He was God, and that He was my Father. He said He would take care of me and that I needed to look to Him all the time. From then on I started living with a sense of His calling and presence in my life. Because of my family life, I didn't really grow up with a strong grounding in the things of God, even though I read the Bible. I didn't have anyone to mentor me or guide me.

I joined the military when I was eighteen and met a person who challenged me in my faith. I really dedicated my life to the Lord at that time. Since I had the time, I did a lot of studying when I was out at sea. I eventually felt a calling to go into the ministry to serve God full time. I went to Columbia Bible College, then to a couple of graduate schools, and finally ended up at Concordia Seminary, where I became a Lutheran pastor.

When I'd been serving at a new parish for just a few months, one of the parishioners called me at about two o'clock in the morning and said he wanted to talk with me. I knew he'd been dealing with some issues, so I agreed to meet him at the church. I went to the church and prayed for guidance about what to say to the man.

My normal habit was to greet people at the door of the church when they arrived and usher them in, since my office was in the back of the building. As I was praying, however, the Lord simply said, "Do not go to the door."

When the man pulled up, I didn't go to the door to greet him. It was unlocked so I was going to just let him come in on his own. He sat in his truck—I could see him through the windows—but I stayed away from the door. He waited in his truck for about twenty minutes before finally coming inside. We talked about the situation, and for some reason he thought I'd said something previously that I hadn't said. He was angry with me, and I had no idea. It took some time, but we were finally able to work through the misunderstanding.

I was able to help him deal with the problems he was having, and we eventually became friends. I helped him come to faith in Jesus, and I baptized him.

About a year later he and I were hanging out one day, just talking. That's when I learned that he'd been in the army, and he had been recognized for marksmanship.

He asked me, "Do you remember that night when we met?"

"Oh yeah. I remember that very well," I said.

"I waited for you in my truck for twenty minutes, but you didn't come out," he said. "I'm glad you didn't because I came there to shoot you that night. I had my rifle in the truck, and I was waiting for you to come out so I could shoot you. Had you appeared in the doorway, I would have shot you."

I said, "Well, I'm thankful you didn't! Normally I would've come out, but I prayed, and God told me not to."

The man had been angry and wrongfully blaming me that night at the church. When I didn't come to the door, he eventually decided to come in and talk to me instead of shooting me. I'm glad I listened to God's voice because if I hadn't, I would have been a goner for sure. With that man's skill with a gun, I would have been a dead man that night! That truly was a divine intervention.

If you aren't sure God exists or that He still intervenes in our lives, I would encourage you to just be totally honest in your heart with God, no matter how you feel, whether angry, happy, frightened, whatever. If you're totally honest with God, He will speak to you. Understand that He'll do that because Jesus Christ has already died for your sins, so He mercifully reaches out to us in our needs as we reach out to Him.

Rev. Richard Jones is a disabled navy veteran and pastor of Grace Lutheran Church by the Sea in Nags Head, North Carolina. Both he and his wife graduated from Columbia Bible College, and they have three sons. For more information, write rjsouthcarolina@gmail.com or visit www.gracelutheranobx.org.

36

Under Construction

Being confident of this very thing, that He
who has begun a good work in you will
complete it until the day of Jesus Christ.

PHILIPPIANS 1:6

*M*Y NAME IS Rick Jordan. I was born in 1948 on Long Island, New York. I'm over sixty years old, and I'm amazed I have lasted this long. Growing up, I always said I'd never live past twenty-one. The reasons will become evident as I share my story.

In school I always sought attention. If someone told me to jump out the school's third floor window or off a bridge, I'd do it, just for attention. I was married while still in high school, and one of the biggest miracles in my life is the fact that we're still married, forty-plus years later.

My best friend was a guy we called "Crazy John." He earned the nickname because he was the type who painted his room black, kept a gun by the door, and said, "They'll never take me alive." We'd drive down the highway at eighty miles per hour, turn the wheel and spin the car, just for fun. You can understand why I didn't think I'd live past twenty-one!

I was with John one day, drinking, carousing, and bar hopping. We were joined by some acquaintances who had something called kief with them. It is a form of hashish. "Try it," they said. "It's better than alcohol. You won't get sick and throw up from it." So we tried it and I liked it—a lot.

I was hanging out the car window, laughing, and having a blast thanks to the hash, so I asked if I could buy some. They tried to find some for me but were unable to and found marijuana instead. I'd never had marijuana, but I decided to buy some—and bought an entire pound! The average person starting out with pot does not buy a pound.

But it was typical of me. I used to go to extremes with everything, whether drinking or drugs. This led me to experiment with LSD, peyote, and opium mixed with hashish. I was drinking a pint of Romana Sambuca liqueur daily and doing as many drugs as I could. I was literally killing myself.

I actually was very sick, but I didn't realize it. I had problems with my teeth and gum infections related to mononucleosis, which I didn't know I had at the time. I went to the dentist and had sweet air (nitrous oxide) for the first time. I did not know I was allergic to it. The reaction I had put me in a coma, during which time I had a spiritual experience.

I found myself in a whirlpool with what seemed like everyone in the world. I started falling, but as I was going through this whirlpool, or tunnel, I'd never felt peace like I felt then. All the weight of my body was removed. I heard awesome music, unlike anything on earth.

At the end of my journey I came before a light. I knew who the light was. Undoubtedly it was Jesus. My face was on the ground, but I could still see Him. He said, "Rick, you can make it." I was amazed. First of all, He knew my name. Second, didn't He know *who* I was? How that very day I'd been doing drugs and other stupid things?

I asked, "How can a person like me—who has done so many bad things—make it, Lord?"

Jesus spoke one word: "Love." When He said it, I actually awoke from the coma. The problem was, I didn't know what love was. I don't remember my parents ever saying they loved me.

For about a year after that experience, even though I knew I'd come into God's presence, I continued with the drinking and drugs. I wound up in the hospital with mononucleosis, then on welfare because I couldn't return to work. I was in my early twenties and married with three children.

Being on welfare was demeaning. I felt like my life wasn't worth living. My experience with God didn't change my life. I was empty.

I decided to kill myself. I went for a walk to think about what to do. I figured throwing myself in front of a train would be a fast, sure way to die. I was on my way to the train tracks to commit suicide, when I walked by a Catholic church. I was raised Catholic and taught through confirmation classes. But the only time I returned was on holidays and special occasions. I wasn't a practicing Catholic.

As I walked by the church, I thought, "If the doors are open, and there's nobody inside, I'll go in and say my last words before I die." Sure enough, it was open and nobody was inside. I went in, knelt down, and for the first time was honest with God. I said, "God, if You *are* real, and the thing that happened to me a year ago was real, and if You *can* do something with this life, then You have to let me know *now*, because it's over. I've had enough. I don't want to live anymore."

Suddenly I heard the same voice that spoke to me during the coma. He clearly said, "Rick, go home."

I said, "OK." I went home and sat in my living room, rather than going to the railroad tracks. I looked up and prayed, "God, now what? I'm home. What are You going to show me here that will change my life?"

"Open the newspaper," He said.

I grabbed the paper but didn't open it; I literally threw it onto the table in front of me, and it opened to the page God intended for it to. It was an article in *Newsday* with a headline that said, "Apollo 15 Astronauts Have Contact With God on the Moon, and Astronaut James Irwin Quits the Astronaut Program and Becomes a Minister."

I remember watching the Apollo 15 mission when it was broadcast on television. During the telecast, while the astronauts were walking on the moon, they lost transmission for about ten minutes. I later learned that's when they had an encounter with God and James Irwin heard the Lord speak to Him.

This was the first thing the Lord showed me that day when I was going to commit suicide. Thereafter God kept showing me *many* miracles. I grew closer to Him as time progressed.

Jesus gave me a new life. I now have a television ministry. My production company produces twenty-eight Christian television programs. People all over the world watch us on cable and on the Internet.

I never thought I'd reach the age I am now. God isn't finished with me yet. I want to make a sign that says "Under Construction" and hang it around my neck. We're all works in progress. All I can say is, "Have mercy on me, Lord, until I get there!"

Rick Jordan is the president and founder of His Reality Ministries, which produces a variety of Christian television programs. He and his wife have three grown children and live on Long Island, New York. For more information, write hisrealitytv@yahoo.com.

37

Civil War and the Evangelist

And I, if I am lifted up from the
earth, will draw all men to Myself.

JOHN 12:32, NAS

*M*Y NAME IS Steven Sebyala. I'm from Africa. I've seen God do miracles throughout my life and my many years in ministry. The fact that I survived my childhood and was called into evangelistic ministry is a miracle in itself.

I was born in 1966 and grew up in Kampala, Uganda. My parents separated and abandoned me when I was a few years old. I never experienced parental love and often regretted where I was born. I grew up on the street in a miserable way, eating whatever I could find on the road. I worked very hard from my youth onward, doing odd jobs just so I could eat and put myself through school. The first time I ever wore shoes was when I was about fourteen years old. Life was hard and meaningless growing up with nobody loving me.

I had little desire to live and seemingly no future. I went from one problem and crisis to another. At one point my uncle, who was a witch, took me in and tried to raise me. I learned much about witchcraft from watching my uncle commune with spirits, cast incantations, and so on.

We had many civil wars in Uganda and multiple governments, one after the next. Idi Amin came to power when I was young, and as a teen I remember having to run and hide often. We got used to hearing shooting and fighting.

During this time, I began searching for answers to many questions in my life, wondering why life was like this. By the grace of God, my friend had a Bible. I borrowed it and started reading it. I loved all I read. While

161

I was reading the New Testament, the war was really intensifying, with much fighting and death.

One morning in 1984 I read Romans 10:9: "If you confess with your mouth the Lord Jesus and believe in your heart that God has raised Him from the dead, you will be saved." I believed, and that day I confessed Jesus as my Lord and Savior.

Growing up in the war environment led me to seek God for my life, because many of my friends were being killed. You would see someone one day, and they would be dead the next. The rebels would siege the city, then the government troops would arrest whomever they could. I was arrested several times on my way to or from school.

Whenever the troops saw a group of boys, they would assume we were rebels fighting the government and would round us up and put us on a truck to be taken away. On two occasions God protected me as I tried to escape. There were about a hundred of us on the truck. As we jumped off and began running, the soldiers began shooting. On the first occasion, one of my friends was shot dead, and another was wounded. The second time, two of my friends were killed as we were fleeing, and again they didn't shoot me. I began to sense God's protection, and read the Bible and prayed even more. I started attending a Pentecostal church, which helped me grow in faith.

One day soldiers surrounded the area where I was. The battle lasted six hours, and they killed many people. When the soldiers left, we went out to bury our friends. I began to regret that I had survived. Why didn't they shoot me? Seeing all my friends dead, and burying them, was difficult. That memory is still very vivid.

Soon after we buried our friends, those killers returned to the area, and we ran. Crossing the roads as we ran, we found hundreds of people dead on the ground. We were being shot at, so in order to survive, we fell among the bodies and pretended to be dead. The soldiers walked among the bodies, stepping on them to see if any were alive. If someone moved, the soldiers would shoot. By the grace of God they never came to me. After several hours I fled.

Witnessing all the fighting and death, I'd ask, "God, why does this happen?" I would have to jump over sometimes fifty bodies every morning as we ran for our lives. Life was rough, but throughout everything God was close to us.

Finally the war ended. The government troops, who had been massacring people, were defeated. This ushered in our current government, which has been in power for more than twenty years. Presently we live in peace.

My father and more than thirty of my other family members died during the war. I later went to the place where they were killed. It was a heap of bones—thousands of bones stacked together in a huge pile. I sat within the piles and picked up some bones. I was bitter and asked God, "Why did they die here like this?"

As I held those bones in my hands, I heard a voice. "Steven!" it said. I looked around, but nobody was there. The voice again said, "Steven Sebyala!"

I wondered if I was hearing demons or spirits of the dead calling me. I had grown up hearing spirits talking because of my uncle and all the witchcraft to which I had been exposed. When I answered the voice, I felt God's peace penetrating my heart and my tears being wiped away.

This loud, audible voice said, "Steven, can you tell which of these bones was rich and which was poor? Can you tell which bone was educated and which wasn't? Which bone had a car or a job? Which bone was which tribe or which color?"

"No, Lord. I cannot tell anything."

In love He spoke to me: "Learn and reach My people before they reach this stage."

At that point I put aside all my own ambitions and began seeking the Lord. That is when God ushered me into the evangelistic ministry that I am doing today. I founded Africa Harvest Mission. I have committed my life to seeing Africa won for Christ. I am fully persuaded from seeing what I saw—and the fact that I didn't die—that I cannot die until I am brought home by the providence of God. I pray for God's Holy Spirit to empower me in Africa. I believe the gospel is the power of God that can bring salvation, and as we preach the gospel, I believe Africa will be saved.

The Lord told me, "If you lift Me up, I'll do what I can do through your life." He does great things in our lives when we lift Him up. Throughout my many years of ministry I have seen miraculous healings, demons being cast out of people, and even the dead being raised. Jesus isn't complicated—He's the same yesterday, today, and forever. He can do anything for anybody.

Steven Sebyala is the founder of Africa Harvest Mission, an evangelistic ministry dedicated to sharing the gospel with the people of Africa. He is also the founder and senior pastor of Calvary Temple Worship Centre, a steadily growing church in the heart of Kampala, Uganda. Steven and his wife, Sara, have five children, as well as five adopted children. As a way to care for children in need, they started a child-care ministry under Africa Harvest Mission called Bridges for Kids, which helps to sponsor more than three hundred kids with food, clothing, education, and medical attention. For more information, write sebyalas@gmail.com or visit www.ahm.us.com.

38

The Seventh Messenger

Be strong and of good courage; do not
be afraid, nor be dismayed, for the LORD
your God is with you wherever you go.

JOSHUA 1:9

*M*Y NAME IS Orlando Crespo. I was born in 1963 into a
Puerto Rican Catholic family in Springfield, Massachusetts. I'd like to
relate a divine intervention that directed me in my calling as a Latino
minister.

In my sophomore year of college I was baptized, and I wanted to be
discipled and mentored seriously. I attended a wonderful church called
Bethany Assembly of God in Agawam, Massachusetts. They had evening
services and youth programs in which I wanted to be involved.

That summer I got a job at a company in Westfield, Massachusetts, and
worked the evening shift, from 3:30 p.m. to 11:30 p.m. My schedule disappointed me, however, because I wouldn't be able to get the discipling and
community that I wanted at church.

I was sad about it one evening as I read my Bible during my break. My
coworker Bob (not his real name) saw me reading and challenged me.
"Why do you believe the Bible?" he asked. "That stuff is just a myth."

I felt I needed to defend the Bible and my faith, and I (politely) rose to
the occasion. Suddenly he said, "I'm kidding. I'm actually a committed
Christian. I was testing you to see if you were committed to Christ." I felt
like hitting him (but, of course, I didn't).

After that incident we became friends. Bob began discipling me. Every
break we'd sit together and read the Scriptures. He started helping me
understand what it meant to be a witness for Christ. I loved God and

wanted to live for Him, but I had no sense of evangelism or caring for the salvation of others. That was challenging for me because as a Catholic there wasn't a real emphasis then on evangelism and being a "witnessing Christian."

As we studied scripture, I got excited about learning to share my faith graciously and lovingly, in a way that could captivate people's hearts without bashing them with the truth of the gospel.

Eventually Bob said, "You're ready for us to go and do some evangelism."

We decided to go out one evening after our shift. We drove to a small downtown area in Westfield, Massachusetts, at about 12:30 a.m. Most people would probably assume two young men out that late would be up to no good, so I had my reservations. We prayed, however, and Bob was confident that God would reveal the person for us to talk to. As he prayed, I thought, "How can he have that much faith that God, at this time of night, would lead us to the right person?" We then waited.

Several people passed by. Whenever I suggested we talk to them, Bob said, "No. Those aren't the ones." This happened multiple times, until one gentleman passed our car walking on the sidewalk, and finally Bob said, "That's the guy!"

We exited the car and as we approached, I could sense the man was hesitant, probably wondering, "What do these guys want?" But he relaxed some when Bob started talking to him.

Bob began sharing with him about Jesus, and we could tell he didn't seem to understand. He looked Latino, so I asked him in Spanish if he understood us. He acknowledged that he was Latino and didn't understand much English.

Bob said, "Orlando, you need to present the gospel to him in Spanish."

That was one of my biggest fears—not just presenting the gospel, which I was still learning to do, but sharing it in Spanish, which was not my native language. My parents would laugh when I spoke Spanish growing up—not to be mean but because sometimes I made funny mistakes. Consequently I was really hesitant about speaking Spanish.

I started talking to him in Spanish and presented the gospel. As we spoke, he began to relax and become attentive to what I was sharing about Christ. It amazed me that he was even interested. I thought, "Wow!

Maybe the Holy Spirit is working." We continued conversing, and it was an awesome time. I asked, "What do you think about what I'm sharing?"

He said, "It's amazing—there were *six other people* who spoke to me today about Jesus. You are the seventh, but you're the only one who actually spoke to me in my native language." He was so shocked; I think he realized God was trying to break through to him and tell him who Christ is.

When I heard about the other people, I started bursting with excitement and a real sense of the Holy Spirit's presence. It became a very special moment in which God dwelt with us. I was probably speaking my best Spanish, the guy understood, and Jesus Christ captivated him.

"The gospel requires a response," I finally said. "God wants us to ask Him for forgiveness through Christ, to accept Him into our lives, embrace His salvation, and verbally acknowledge that. Are you willing to pray a prayer of repentance and ask God to come into your life to dwell in you?"

"Yes," he said. "I think God is trying to talk to me." We then prayed together. He was really moved, thanking me several times. We gave him a gospel tract and suggested he read it. I gave him my information and told him if he wanted to talk more, he could call me. We said good-bye, and he left.

I had translated for Bob as we went along, so he had a sense of what was happening. We were elated from seeing God's Spirit at work. Bob was ecstatic that this was something I could do, after being led by God to train me, then seeing results the first time we went out.

For me it was a mark of God's divine direction, a turning point, and a gift from the Spirit. After that encounter God said to me, "Orlando, I have called you to be a minister of the gospel. I have set your life as a light for this." My background and ability to speak Spanish would become part of my ministry.

It was around 1984 when I shared the gospel with that man, and now more than twenty-five years later, I'm doing what God gave me to do at that moment—ministering the gospel to Latinos. In 2000 I became director of InterVarsity Christian Fellowship's Latino ministry. This is my calling, and we're seeing wonderful things happen on college campuses.

We minister to more than nineteen hundred Latino students who are actively involved in our ministries throughout America. Much of this originated from that divine moment when God set the course of my life in ministry. It happened so that man would get saved but also to bring about God's direction and the course my life should take. That night was a divine intervention that has influenced my life ever since.

Rev. Dr. Orlando Crespo is director of InterVarsity Christian Fellowship's Latino ministry, LaFe, and has been with InterVarsity for more than twenty years. He is also a founding pastor of New Life in The Bronx Church, in the New York City borough. He and his wife live in the Bronx, and they have two grown sons. For more information, write Orlando.Crespo2@gmail.com or visit www.intervarsity.org/lafe.

39

Saved From Certain Death

The fear of the LORD is a fountain of life, to
turn one away from the snares of death.

PROVERBS 14:27

*M*Y NAME IS John Kruse. I was born in Queens, New York, in 1966. My wife, Sharon and I currently live with our children in Dutchess County, New York. I'm going to tell you about a divine intervention in my life (one of many) that led me, as I was seeking God, to commit my life to Jesus.

By 1996 I was living near my current residence in Poughkeepsie, New York. I'd been seeking God at that point in my life. Some things were tugging at my heart, and I was questioning many things, wondering, "Is God there? Is He real?" I was also seeking ways of understanding people and reading self-studies on psychology and self-help books, such as Norman Vincent Peale's *The Power of Positive Thinking*.

One day I got into a conversation with a pastor I'd met at my mother-in-law's house. When I told him what I was reading, he posed a question to me. "You seem to have some knowledge there, but you're not really reading the Bible, right?"

"No, not really," I said.

"Well, why not go to the source of what these people are saying?" he asked. "Why not go to the source and read that book, which is God's book, the Bible?"

I agreed and wondered what was in it. I started perusing the Bible and watching *The 700 Club* a little bit. I was pondering what life was about. We were quite poor and had had many catastrophes in our lives. I would say at that point I wasn't paying a lot of attention to spiritual things—I was only beginning my quest. Then an incident occurred that was a big attention getter.

At the time I had a big pickup truck. The front tires were bald; the treads were worn out. One day I was on my way to my college class. It was raining, and the roads were slippery. I descended a big hill on Barmore Road, near my home. At the bottom of the hill and around a bend, the road intersected with Route 82, a major roadway where traffic typically traveled at around fifty-five miles per hour. I wasn't paying attention as I came down the hill. As I reached the end of the road and rounded the bend, I hit the brakes, but the truck didn't stop. I began skidding down the hill. I was going too fast.

As I came to the intersection I looked to the right, down Route 82, and saw a car coming. It was on the other side of the road in the far lane. I thought, "Well, maybe I'll get out into the near lane, and I'll be fine. They'll be able to go around me." But then I looked to the left, and in the near lane was a big eighteen-wheel tractor-trailer truck barreling toward the intersection.

It was stunning—I remember feeling utter fear and thinking, "I'm going to die." I took my hands off the steering wheel and covered up, trying to brace for the impact. I didn't watch as I waited for the inevitable. Suddenly, I felt quiet—dead silence. It was eerie. No tires screeching, no horns honking—nothing. I actually thought I'd died. I thought, "Wow...that was painless."

As I looked up, everything was still. I looked to the left and saw the rear end of the car driving down the road. I looked to the right and saw the back of the eighteen-wheeler traveling down the other end of the road. When I looked down, I saw that my truck was entirely across the near lane. It was a big pickup truck with a long bed and king cab. When I looked down by the driver's door, I saw that it was even with the double yellow lines on the road, so the front end of the truck was into the far lane about three quarters of the way.

I have no explanation for why the other vehicles didn't hit me. I thought when I took cover that I was definitely going to be hit by one vehicle or the other, or maybe both. The experience really shook me. I knew instantly I'd just experienced a miracle, or a divine intervention, because there was no way those vehicles could've missed me. There wasn't enough room on the road. I remember pulling my truck over to the side of the road, trembling, crying, and thanking the Lord.

"OK, You *do* exist," I told Him. That experience changed my life. I don't know how He did it, but God saved me from certain injury or death.

If you don't know Jesus, my message to you is to give Him a chance. Wait on Him to show Himself to you. He is real, and He's still working miracles and does care about His children.

John Kruse is an accountant, entrepreneur, and kung fu instructor. He and his wife live in Poughkeepsie, New York, where they are homeschool parents of eleven children. For more information, write kruse15@earthlink.net.

40

True Strength

I can do all things though Christ
who strengthens me.

PHILIPPIANS 4:13

MY NAME IS Jonathan Bernor. I'm an evangelist and champion powerlifter. I love Jesus and enjoy serving Him, but I haven't always. God intervened mightily to bring me to this place in my life.

I was born in 1975 on Long Island, New York. Growing up was rough, and due to a painful childhood I became hard-hearted. Seeking respect and identity as a teenager, I got into crime and drugs. I was so scared by a near-fatal overdose of crack cocaine in 1992 that I quit using and decided to focus only on becoming the "best" dealer I could. I was consumed with the drug culture and the money and power it brought. I continued to perfect my trade into my late teens.

In my early twenties I expanded, developing a large cocaine and marijuana distribution ring, and a huge burglary ring. I was making about $30,000 per week from burglaries. I thought I was hot stuff. They used to call John Gotti "The Teflon Don" because nothing would stick to him. In my own pride and arrogance I felt the same way about myself.

Several times I discovered I was being investigated. I thought it was my connections that were keeping me from getting caught, but I see now it was God's sovereignty. For some reason God kept me from jail. He also saved my life multiple times. I had many close calls. I had weapons drawn on me and run-ins with law enforcement and organized crime. It was a crazy life, but through it all God protected me.

The incident that finally convinced me to submit to God happened in April 1999. I developed weird, intense pains in my stomach. It felt like someone had hit me with a baseball bat. I went to the hospital, and after the doctors ran some tests, they said, "Some things look slightly skewed. You could be dehydrated. Why don't you go home and come back if things don't improve?"

I went home but remained bedridden with horrible pain. There was no improvement. I returned to the hospital and finally was diagnosed with pancreatitis. At that time I didn't know what the pancreas was or what it did. The pancreas is the organ that releases digestive enzymes. With pancreatitis the pancreas basically starts digesting itself. It's extremely painful, and there's little they can do for it.

About 10 percent of people who develop pancreatitis die from it, and those with chronic pancreatitis (like I had) become malnourished because they can't eat. Eating aggravates it. While I was in the hospital, I was fed through IVs and could only eat ice chips. So there I was, twenty-four years old, with lots of money and power—and desperately sick. I was in shock.

I had my pager and cell phone, and I continued dealing drugs and conducting business from my hospital bed. A month passed, and I was in and out of the hospital. Another month passed, and I was still in pain. At age twenty-four, this diagnosis was crippling. It wasn't just because I was facing my own mortality, but also because everything I'd lusted for no longer had value. What did it matter if I made eight grand in a night if I was in agony and couldn't enjoy it? I was bedridden and couldn't enjoy anything.

It was the first time I couldn't talk, fight, or buy my way out of a situation. I was stuck between the proverbial "rock and a hard place." Three months in and out of the hospital, and not a day went by that I was without pain.

My mom is an amazing woman and a tremendous example of Christ's love. All throughout my life, and through that ordeal, she would encourage me to leave my criminal life and follow Jesus.

One day at the hospital they did an ERCP, an endoscopic test in which a scope is put down the throat. I'm a big guy, and they couldn't give me enough tranquilizers to knock me out. I was awake while they were shoving the scope down my throat. After that traumatic experience

I went up to the hospital's midlevel roof and prayed, "God, I can't do this anymore. I'm done. If I'm going to live in pain the rest of my life, whatever it takes, God…I accept You, Jesus, as my Lord and Savior. Now the only thing that matters is You. Please move in my life."

The doctors couldn't determine what was causing the pancreatitis. They called it "idiopathic"—no known cause. I was a healthy twenty-four year old, and it usually happens to people with long histories of alcohol abuse or other problems—none of which I had. They were perplexed and discharged me again.

The next day, amazingly, I had no pain. This was the day after I committed my life to Christ. The second and third days still there was no pain. I didn't tell anyone because I was afraid I would jinx myself. The fourth day out of the hospital I went to dinner with my family. I ate a chicken parmesan dinner. The following day there was no pain! I suddenly *knew* I was healed!

I returned to my wonderful Jewish doctor who I could tell really cared about me. She asked, "How are you feeling?"

I said, "I feel great. Jesus healed me."

She looked at me like I had six heads, but I knew I'd been healed. The pain was gone. It blew my mind. I always knew God existed and that Jesus is the Savior of all mankind, but from then on it became *personal.* I said, "God, I owe You my life." When He intervened with my healing, I turned and gave Him my 110 percent. That was the defining moment in my life.

I left the drug world. I called the people who owed me money from the street and said, "I don't want the money." I destroyed my cocaine and marijuana. I had money that I'd stolen, and I gave it to people from whom I'd stolen. I kept only $700 that was legal, clean money. I enrolled in Youth With A Mission (a Christian youth discipleship program), and that $700 went toward the program's tuition.

Two weeks after I got saved, I began volunteering. I've been in full-time ministry since 1999 and have never looked back.

As of 2013 I've twice been ranked number one in the world for my weight class in powerlifting (in 2008 and 2012), making me one of the strongest men on earth. People have asked me what my definition of true strength is. I can bench press eight hundred pounds and squat a thousand, but that's not true strength. True strength is knowing Jesus Christ died on the cross for my sins and that I'm a weak, sinful man. Like Philippians 4:13 says, "I can do all things through Christ who strengthens me."

Having chased the things of this world much of my life, I can tell you that there's no peace like the peace Jesus gives. Just ask Him if He is real. Ask Him to reveal Himself to you. I know if you're sincere, He'll answer you.

 **Jonathan Bernor** is a world-champion powerlifter who has been twice ranked number one in the world in his weight class. He is also a full-time evangelist, itinerant minister, and public speaker. He lives with his family on Long Island, New York. For more information, write jonathanbernor@gmail.com or follow him on Twitter: @Jonathanbernor.

41

The Miracle of Hannah

Then [Hannah] made a vow and said, "O
Lord of hosts, if You will...give Your
maidservant a male child, then I will
give him to the Lord all the days of his
life...." Then Eli answered and said, "Go
in peace, and the God of Israel grant your
petition which you have asked of Him."

1 Samuel 1:11, 17

My name is Sandra Rivera. I was born in 1965 and raised in a Puerto Rican Catholic family in Springfield, Massachusetts. In 1993, when I was twenty-eight years old, I started noticing that my body was producing breast milk, although I wasn't pregnant.

My sister said, "You should get that checked because that could be a sign of breast cancer." I immediately went and got some tests done.

The doctor called and asked, "When can I see you and your husband?" When she said that, we knew something wasn't right. We went immediately. When the doctor spoke with us, all I remember hearing was "a growth in the pituitary gland."

"Are you saying I have a brain tumor?" I asked.

"Yes," she said. Suddenly, thoughts raced through my head: "How much longer will I live? How will I tell my parents that they will probably outlive me? Who will take care of my husband?" You go through many different emotions.

We saw a neurosurgeon who said that because I was young and it was a risky surgery, they would try to treat it with medication. They also said that I would never be able to conceive because the tumor was causing my body to think I was already pregnant.

I began to wonder what would happen. My husband, Tom, was a born-again Christian. Tom began teaching me about the promises that God has for us in the Bible. Additionally, right after we discovered the tumor, my mom said, "If you want God to do something for you, you should start going to church." I began attending church with my husband and learning about God's promises.

Meanwhile I was taking the medication the doctors prescribed, but it made me feel worse than the actual tumor did. After about a year and a half, I stopped taking it. By then I had given my heart to the Lord and become a born-again Christian. My husband taught me what the Bible says, that by Jesus's "stripes" (the whipping He received) "we were healed" (Isa. 53:5). Not that we *will be* healed, but that we *were* healed. He began teaching me about faith, saying, "There's nothing God can't do."

My husband and our pastor showed me Bible passages that I could apply to my situation, such as Mark 5:25–34, about the woman with the issue of blood who was healed when she touched the hem of Jesus's garment. When she touched Him, Jesus said, "Your faith has made you well" (v. 34). I kept reciting Bible verses about God's promises and healing.

A year and a half after my diagnosis (when I had just stopped taking the medication), I returned to the doctor and was told the tumor was growing. I had been told that the medication might shrink the tumor but that it would never completely disappear without surgery, which they refused to do because of its delicate location.

Around the same time the doctors had told me that I would not be able to conceive, I met a couple who were prophets. The woman told me, "The Lord has said He will give you a child." They knew nothing about me or my medical history.

I thought, "That's crazy!" because the doctors told me I could never have children. Then I thought, "Whom should I believe—the doctors who have the medical background, or this woman who says she hears from God?"

After learning more about God, I chose to believe that God was speaking through this woman. I said, "Lord, if You said it, I'm holding

You to it." I began to believe, and pray, "Father, thank You because although my natural eyes can't see it, I believe in my heart that You have healed me." I began not only to say it, but to also live it.

Friends and coworkers would ask, "How are you feeling?"

I'd say, "Great! I'm healed!"

"You are?" they'd ask.

"Yes. By faith!"

I was always cheerful, and people couldn't believe that I could be feeling so sick and still be joyful. All along I was getting regular scans and blood tests.

In January 1997 I went for another CT scan. As I was lying in the scan machine I kept praising God, saying, "Thank You, Father, for my healing. Thank You because in the worst times of my life, You have never left me. You've always been faithful." I kept praising and thanking Him for being so merciful and compassionate. I felt His presence, like He was there with me.

Suddenly I felt this physical sensation of pressure in the bottom of my feet. It began to move up my body all the way to my head—it felt as if something was being squeezed out of me. I can only describe it as, when you reach the end of a toothpaste tube you squeeze and roll it up from the bottom, and the last bit of toothpaste goes *pop!* as it comes out with a burst of air.

That's what I felt—a pressure from the bottom of my feet moving to the top of my head, and a little *pop!* when it reached my head. I exclaimed, "Oh, Jesus!" I knew He had created the miracle that I had so long believed He had. I kept repeating, "Thank You!" and then I dozed off.

On February 14, 1997, I went back for my test results. The doctor looked at the chart, then looked up at me. He again looked at the chart as if confused, then looked at me again. I asked, "What's wrong?"

He said, "It's gone."

"Thank You, Jesus! Praise God!" I exclaimed.

The test result read, "There is a slit-like cavity where the tumor once sat," which acknowledged that there had been a tumor there, and now there was just a scar. It was as if God removed it and said, "Let Me leave this scar so nobody will doubt where it was."

The Lord not only healed me, but also gave me a child, as promised. My daughter was born in 2002. We named her Hannah, after Samuel's mother in the Bible, who couldn't conceive. When she prayed to the Lord, He gave her a child (1 Sam. 1:8–20). I had another daughter, Olivia, in 2006.

The Lord is faithful. It has been an awesome journey being part of His miracles. You hear about other people's experiences, but when it actually happens to you, it's something entirely different. There were times when I'd say, "I can't believe it!" But it actually happened to me. I've gone for regular follow-ups, and there's no sign of the tumor. God is awesome!

Sandra Rivera describes herself as "a very grateful mother." She lives with her family in Massachusetts, where she works in the health care industry. For more information, write tomsan333@aol.com. To view medical documentation, see Appendix.

42

Shot Between the Eyes

No weapon formed against you shall prosper.

ISAIAH 54:17

*M*Y NAME IS Joshua Bender. I was born in Baltimore, Maryland, in 1974. As an eight-year-old I asked Jesus to be my Lord and Savior after watching an end-times movie at church. Although I was only eight, I realized I was making a big decision. After praying, I felt something new had happened inside me—my "being" was different. I was happy about the change.

Growing up, I had few friends. My mom was single and poor. As a result of moving often, having little structure or stability in my life, watching lots of TV, attending public school, and getting bullied frequently, I became jaded and cynical. I developed many bad attitudes and beliefs. My heart's desire gradually changed from God to worldly things.

I attended high school on Long Island, New York. By senior year I was introverted, angst-ridden, and had a big chip on my shoulder. I didn't want friends; I just wanted to graduate and move to Texas, where I'd spent much of my childhood.

After graduating, I returned to Texas and rented a house with my friend Mark (not his real name).

Mark and his friends smoked pot, and within two weeks of moving to Texas, after never having done drugs, I took my first drag of pot with them. I enjoyed the mellow feeling it gave me. It quickly became a habit, and we all were getting high almost nightly.

Things progressed rapidly from there. Several weeks later our roommate Karl (not his real name), our neighbor Luke (not his real name), and I started burglarizing cars to support our habit. That wasn't working out, however. Since getting high was basically all we lived for, we decided to start growing pot in incubators and dealing it. I planned on getting a gun to protect myself while I was dealing. I was heading straight into stupidity.

On September 15, 1994, Karl, Luke, and I were with some of Luke's friends, teenagers like us. One guy said his neighbor was away, and he knew how to get into his house. He added that this neighbor had a large gun collection that we could steal.

All the guys said, "Yeah!"

As much as I wanted to be part of the crowd, I knew if we got caught we'd go to jail. I wanted to avoid prison, so I decided against going with them. They drove to the house and eventually returned with the guns.

Back at our house the guys were playing with the guns. Karl had a small-caliber pistol, and he'd pulled the clip out, thinking it was empty. He didn't realize someone had cocked the gun, which puts a bullet in the chamber. I was sitting about six feet away, thinking about getting high.

Karl started messing around, pointing the gun at me, saying, "Hey dude, I'm going to shoot you." I ignored him. He continued brandishing the gun saying, "Dude, I'm going to shoot you!" I brushed him off and told him to get the gun out of my face.

He repeated the threat and pulled the trigger. I honestly don't think he knew the gun was loaded, but it fired, and I was shot between the eyes. I was knocked off my chair onto my back. Totally dazed, I tried to sit up but kept falling back down. I didn't know what was happening. I eventually realized everyone had fled the room. Not knowing what had occurred, they just heard a gunshot and bolted.

So I was lying there, alone, bleeding profusely from a gunshot wound to the head. The bullet entered between my eyes, on the bridge of my nose. I touched my nose, and when I took my hand away, there was blood everywhere. I then put two and two together and figured I'd been shot. I didn't know what to do. I actually yelled to the guys, "I'm not dead yet! Call an ambulance!"—and they did. They brought me towels, helped me sit up, and started telling me what to say to the cops.

The guys wanted me to lie and say some stranger had shot me and fled. They didn't want to get caught with stolen guns. In my dazed state I agreed. They hid the guns behind the house, and I started praying.

When the police arrived and questioned me, something told me to tell the truth, and I did. I pointed to Karl, the guy who shot me, and told them what happened and about the guns in the back yard. I didn't want to be implicated in their crimes. I hadn't stolen anything—I was innocent and ended up shot.

Eventually I was loaded into an ambulance, where I started to think I would die. I'd never heard of anyone surviving a point-blank gunshot to the head. Maybe once in a great while, but no doubt 99 percent will die.

This bullet didn't just graze my scalp; it actually went into my head. I started praying for my mother, asking God to help her deal with this.

I also prayed, "Lord, I know I've been living like a complete reprobate, in sin, but if You save me, I promise to live for You." When you're at death's door, the lies you tell yourself evaporate, and you become truthful—you fully recognize the condition of your heart. I understood that because of

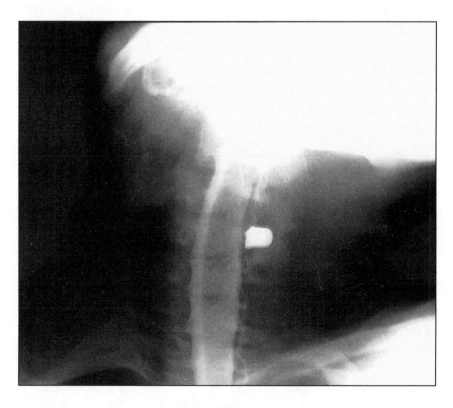

my painful childhood, I had many issues to work through. I knew there were certain things I had to live through and lessons I had to learn the hard way, but I told the Lord I would do my best to serve Him.

At the hospital they hooked me up to an IV to give me blood to replace what I'd lost. Once I was stabilized, they took multiple CT scans, which revealed that the bullet was in the back of my neck. It somehow went through my sinuses and exited in front of my brain. I was shot between the eyes, and the bullet should've gone straight into my cerebellum, leaving me a vegetable. It basically exited into my brain cavity but didn't touch my brain, then "magically" ended up in the back of my neck. The doctors couldn't explain how that happened.

The doctor who took the CT scans said, "I'm going back to church. There's no way the bullet could have ended up in the back of your neck. It doesn't make sense." He thought it was a miracle. This was a small-caliber bullet, but even given its size, it should've hit something—but it didn't.

I don't know how God did it; I just know He did because it defies any laws of reality that we know. God showed up!

I was released from the hospital after ten days. That miraculous event led me to eventually return to my faith and become a conscientious disciple of Christ. The Lord took away my angst and worry and gave me peace. I'm happy now. Jesus is good! I'm so thankful He saved me and healed my life!

Joshua Bender is a graphic artist, t-shirt designer, and entrepreneur who lives with his wife and daughter in Southern California. For more information, write seraphimvi@yahoo.com.

43

God's Voice in the Midst of the Storm

Obey My voice, and do according
to all that I command you.

JEREMIAH 11:4

*M*Y NAME IS Gwen Fazzina. I was born in Queens, New York, in 1939. I'm going to relate a story to you—one of many in my life that seem to have no logical explanation, except possibly that they were the result of angels intervening in my life or God warning me about certain things.

This particular incident happened in October 1973 during a big thunderstorm. Outside it wasn't fit for man or beast—it was windy, tree limbs were coming down, there was lightning, and it was pouring rain. My family and I were finishing dinner in our home in Yaphank, New York. I was loading the dishwasher when suddenly a voice, with no emotion, went through my head and said, "Go check Grandma's house." My grandma lived in New York City, but she had a summer home several towns away from us in Mastic Beach.

"That's weird," I thought, as I dismissed it and continued with the dishes.

Suddenly it came back. "Go check Grandma's house." At the time, my parents were staying in the city, so the house was empty.

Looking outside at the nasty weather, I asked my husband, "Would you like to take a ride with me to Mastic Beach?"

"Are you crazy? Look at the stormy night out there. I'm not going out in this weather."

"OK," I said. But something kept bugging me to go. I asked my teenage sons, and of course they didn't want to go out in the storm either.

I was getting agitated because something kept telling me, "Go look. Go look."

Finally my oldest daughter, Janine, said, "I'll go with you, Mom."

So we started out in the horrific weather. We could hardly get through the streets. Tree limbs were down; the torrential downpour was still going. When we got to my grandmother's street we drove past her house and saw nothing unusual—only rain and the wind swirling like crazy.

We turned around and went back up the street past her house a second time, but something was telling me that I had to go back and look again. "I still can't leave here," I told Janine.

"Well, we looked and there's nothing happening," she said.

"I have to check again," I said.

We turned around at the end of the block and went back a third time. Still we saw nothing. We turned around again to go home. This time, I drove really slowly down the block, and as we looked at my grandmother's house, we suddenly saw a bright, white light on the neighbor's house next door. "What the heck was that?" we wondered aloud.

When we looked closer, we realized the house was on fire! We had to turn around and try to find a house that had a phone because those were summer homes, and not all of them have telephones. The man down the block on the corner had one. He called the fire department and police, who responded and the fire was put out.

We saved the neighbor's house, and the owner was very thankful we were there. We had to call him in Queens to come out. His house had minimal damage, but if we hadn't been there, it would have burned to the ground because nobody was around.

Apparently the house was struck by lightning, which set it on fire. We just "happened" to be there exactly when the fire started.

Looking back, it was funny, because we tried to leave several times, and I kept saying, "No, I have to go back again and look." I really believe the voice I heard must have been God saying, "Hey, get over there and check this out." We had no idea why we were there or why we had to go. There was an urgency in my heart, but also a calm. The urgency I felt

185

wasn't like, *"Hurry up and get over there!"* The voice that I heard say, "Go check Grandma's house," was calm.

That type of thing has happened to me a lot. A strong, calm thought just passes through my head, and if I ignore it, it's usually not good. So I listened to it that night, and we saved the neighbor's house. Thank God! I've had many other instances of divine intervention in my life, as have other people. Many people just don't recognize God's intervention in their lives.

Be aware and be thankful. God is in control!

Gwen Fazzina was born in Queens, New York, and now lives on Long Island with Joe, her husband of more than forty years. She is an active member of the Mastic Peninsula Historical Society and Grace Lutheran Church in Mastic Beach, New York. For more information, write fazzina@earthlink.net.

44

Delivered From Witchcraft

He who dwells in the secret place
of the Most High shall abide under
the shadow of the Almighty.
PSALM 91:1

*M*Y NAME IS Penny Kassay. I was born in 1970 on Long Island, New York. I began following Jesus in 1991 after years of turmoil that led me into a life of witchcraft. My childhood was hard. I started using drugs at age fourteen. My parents separated, and thereafter I was sexually abused. I hardened and rebelled against my mother.

At sixteen I told God, "If You want me, then You need to come get me, because You've never done anything for me." A month later someone came to my door and said I should come to church and that I needed to know Jesus.

"That's good for you," I said, "but I'm gonna live the life I want to live."

I partied often until I met my first boyfriend. By age seventeen we were living together. After almost a year together I learned he was a warlock. He had cut himself with knives. I thought I was seeing a demoniac who needed an exorcism (like Linda Blair from the movie *The Exorcist*). He'd show me things he could do with witchcraft. We entered a spiritual realm I didn't know existed.

I'd always been curious about witchcraft. During my rebellious teenage years, many people told me they could see me being powerful in witchcraft and that I should get into it, which I ultimately did.

One time my boyfriend said, "Let's commit suicide and die right now."

"No way!" I said. "What about heaven?"

The television wasn't on, and we didn't have the remote control for it, but suddenly the TV turned on and I heard the word *heaven*. On-screen was a PTL (Praise the Lord) Network broadcast. I saw preachers talking about heaven. That was my first experience with God, though I didn't realize it at the time.

My boyfriend went insane from the amount of occultism he'd entered into. The occult will drive you crazy. We separated and I moved on.

My life was a *living hell* when I was in the occult. I'd walk around fearful, not knowing what would happen to me. I was writing spells, performing incantations, and would even speak in a weird, ungodly language.

With witchcraft, you actually make a covenant with demons—though you may not realize it. You think *you* are the one doing supernatural things through the dark practices (for example, moving your spirit into animals in order to see what's happening around you). But it's not you—it's demonic spirits operating through you.

This may sound like I'm off the deep end, but I'm really not. I have a very normal life today. But when I was into witchcraft, life was terrifying, and I didn't understand what was happening. I thought I was doing all those powerful things—until the day I realized I couldn't control it.

A turning point came when I was about age twenty. A friend and I were watching TV one night when, just like my ex-boyfriend, he revealed to me that he was into witchcraft. Then he said, "I don't want to watch this anymore," and he changed the channel. When he did, I saw horrifying, hellish images of bloody people, and worse. It was scary.

I started feeling sick, like you'd feel from the nausea and headaches that accompany the flu. My body started tingling, and I lost my equilibrium. I began fainting, off and on, and fell down repeatedly. I went from one end of my house to the other, finally ending up on my bedroom floor, semiconscious.

Suddenly I was falling down a dark tunnel and couldn't stop. It was the scariest feeling—as if I'd jumped off a cliff and there was nowhere to land. At that moment I knew I was dying and headed for hell. I thought, "Oh, God, I don't want my family to find me dead." I didn't want them to know I'd been involved in witchcraft, and that it had failed me. My strength and everything I believed in had failed me.

Then something inside me clicked. I said, "Jesus, please! I'll serve You! Help me, Jesus!" *Immediately* I was back in my body. It was the most powerful—not wonderful—but incredible, life-transforming experience I'd ever had!

I got up, asking, "What just happened to me?" My friend was gone; he'd left me to die by myself. That's typical of witchcraft: when you enter the occult realm you can't trust anyone. The Bible says that Satan "prowls around like a roaring lion, seeking someone to devour" (1 Pet. 5:8, NAS). Satan wanted to devour me, but God intervened.

Later another friend and I went to a psychic who had been mentoring me. She didn't know what had just happened to me; I hadn't told her anything. She told my friend things about her future, but she wouldn't say anything to me except, "Talk to Jesus." I was getting angry with her. Usually psychics will tell you what you want to hear. All she could say to me that day was, "Talk to Jesus."

I went home and said to God, "I know You're real. I know You want me to serve You, but I don't know how. Show me the way. Lord, if Your power is real, then You need to help me overcome this witchcraft." The witchcraft had returned, but I was no longer torturing others with it; it was now torturing me.

One night I could feel demons leaping on me. I couldn't see them, but I felt them jumping on me and pulling on me, harassing me. I could hear them mocking me and laughing. I wasn't insane—this actually happened. Later I learned from other people that similar things had happened to them.

I asked God, "Why is this happening? If Satan has all this power, where's Your power?" Within a week, I found out.

On January 1, 1991, I walked into the Jesus Is Lord church in Holtsville, New York, and saw a man all dressed in white who resembled an angel. I saw a purplish cloud, like smoke, inside the church. I couldn't believe what I was seeing.

I stopped and stood, stunned in the hallway, just looking. Then the man said to me, "This is a great church. It's filled with the Holy Spirit." I told him I could tell. I sat in the back row and enjoyed the service.

Through the music and preaching I could feel God's power working in me. I accepted Christ into my life, and things started changing.

I continued attending regularly. Within a week I stopped smoking and eliminated other bad things from my past. After three weeks I took all my occult things (a tray of crystal balls and tarot cards) and trashed them.

God delivered me and changed my life. I had been miserable, filled with fear, worry, and self-doubt. God took all that away. Now I have joy and peace, and I'm so grateful. What I have today is supernatural—but divine.

No matter how deeply you're into the occult—even if you've sold your soul—Jesus can deliver you. He did it for me, and He can do it for you.

Penny Kassay is senior business intermediary for Gottesman Company, one of the nation's largest mergers and acquisitions firms. She lives on Long Island, New York, with her family. For more information, write penelopedymonds@yahoo.com. Find her on Facebook at "Beloved2ny" or on Twitter @Beloved1ny.

45

We Need a Place to Land!

Blessed be the LORD, because He has
heard the voice of my supplications! The
LORD is my strength and my shield; my
heart trusted in Him, and I am helped.

PSALM 28:6–7

$\mathcal{M}$Y NAME IS Grant Stubbs. I was born in Foxton, New Zealand, in 1961, and raised in a Christian home. My father was a minister. Growing up, we moved often, as my father was posted at different churches. We ended up in Blenheim, a small town in Marlborough at the top of New Zealand's South Island, where I've lived for more than twenty years. My parents moved on, but I stayed, married, and now have children of my own.

As a teen I was involved with Youth for Christ, an organization founded in America that's also strong in New Zealand. I attended a Campus Life club, where I committed my life to Jesus at age fifteen. I later became a Youth for Christ leader and helped run a Campus Life club.

I've experienced many divine interventions in my life. One such amazing instance happened in 2008. For my birthday that year my wife gave me a voucher for a flight with a friend, Owen, in a microlight airplane. I was grateful for the gift because I love flying. I'd been up with Owen once before and really enjoyed it. Owen is an air force mechanic, and this microlight belonged to the Air Force Flying Club, so Owen had access to it.

It was after church one Sunday in May (late autumn in New Zealand) when Owen asked, "Would you like to take our flight this afternoon?"

"Sounds good!" I said.

It was a stunningly beautiful, crystal-clear, windless autumn day as we headed to the airfield. We checked over the plane and made sure we had enough petrol (gas). This microlight had an enclosed cockpit, like a miniature Cessna. The seating area is very tight, and we were jammed against each other. The petrol goes in a big plastic tank behind where you sit. It doesn't have a fuel gauge, only a strip gauge so you can see how much fuel is going in. We calculated how much fuel we needed and how far we were going, then put the fuel in and took off.

We flew up the Wairau Valley in Blenheim. Then we flew over the vineyards and mountains to Nelson, a coastal city with beautiful beaches. We flew for about forty-five minutes before turning and starting for home.

We crossed Tasman Bay, a huge body of water in the Nelson area. On the other side of Tasman Bay is a range of steep hills and mountainous terrain. This was in the Marlborough Sounds, where there are thousands of bays and coves, but unlike on the Nelson side, not many beaches. It's isolated country, with rugged bush and a rocky coastline.

As we approached the Marlborough Sounds, we needed more altitude to climb over one of the mountain ranges. We were starting our climb when the microlight's motor suddenly sputtered and cut out! Owen restarted it, the propeller spun for several seconds, then stopped again.

"Owen, what is it?"

"Grant, we've run out of petrol."

"What would you like me to do?"

"Just pray!" he said.

So I immediately began to pray loudly, "Lord, please help us get over that steep ledge!" If we weren't able to clear that ledge, we would plow into the side of the hill and be killed. You don't crash a microlight and walk away from it. We would've disappeared into the rugged bush, and possibly not have been found for some time.

As I prayed, the motor kept sputtering and suddenly fired up again! Owen was fiddling with the controls, trying to keep it going, and it gave us just enough power to clear the ridge! Then, as soon as we were over the ridge, it cut out completely.

We were at about twenty-five hundred feet with no power, over a very isolated part of the sound. I prayed, "Lord, we need to find somewhere to land!"

Later Owen told me, "Grant, I thought I knew where all the emergency landing strips were in the Marlborough Sounds and had marked them on my maps, but as far as I had seen, there were none near us. We were in big trouble."

As I prayed, we desperately looked around, trying to spot a place to land. We just cleared the ridge, and when I looked over my shoulder, I spotted, down at the head of this little bay, a long, narrow meadow squeezed between two ridges. We realized we could land there! Owen did a fine piece of gliding, turning the plane around and guiding us to this meadow, which had a steep angle in toward the bay. It was very difficult to maneuver into, but he got us down and we landed safely.

When we came to a stop, we both let out a big, "*Whoopee!* Thank You, Lord!" We were very relieved.

When I opened the door to get out, I saw a huge water pump tower beside our plane. There was a big sign on the tower that read, "Jesus Is Lord." We started laughing. For us that was absolute confirmation that God had answered our prayers, enabling us to clear that ridge and find somewhere to land. If that isn't a *sign* from God, I don't know what is!

After several minutes a young couple came wandering down a little pathway toward us. They introduced themselves as Truth and Grace, saying, "Welcome to our farm." We learned that we'd landed on an organic farm owned by Christians. They gave us some fuel for our plane. We spent some time with them, talking, praying, and thanking the Lord for saving our lives that day. Then we nervously turned the plane around, pulled it back as far as we could so we had as long a runway as possible, took off, and managed to get home.

Another amazing thing about this is that the farm covered two hundred acres, but the only flat area was the meadow where we landed. The farmers told us ordinarily that little flat area was where all their livestock graze. They had cows, sheep, deer, donkeys, emus, ostriches, and pigs. For some reason, when we were coming in to land, all the animals had moved to the side. The little landing area was completely clear so we could land safely.

That was another miracle. Normally, the animals would have been in the way and wouldn't have moved because they wouldn't have heard us coming, since we were gliding in without power. If they'd been in the meadow, we could have plowed into them, which would have been disastrous for such a tiny plane. It was a miracle that the animals were off the "runway."

The farmers had erected the sign on the tower to celebrate the World Day of Prayer. Evidently God protected us and didn't want us to check out just yet! It was truly a divine intervention! I hope this testimony encourages you to know that God is real, and that He loves His children.

Grant Stubbs (right) owns a Caltex fuel station in Blenheim, a small town in Marlborough at the top of the South Island of New Zealand. He and his wife, Jenni, have been married more than twenty-seven years and have three teenage children.

Owen Wilson or "OB," as he is called (left), is a retired air force aircraft mechanic who now teaches aircraft engineering to civilian personnel in New Zealand. He and his wife, Angela, are the parents of twins, John and Sharon.

Grant and OB remain good friends, sharing a common love of motor sports. They live in the same town and are both very involved in their churches. For more information, write to Grant Stubbs at stubz@xtra.co.nz or Owen Wilson at ob.angels@live.com.

46

Love and Faith in Action

For assuredly, I say to you, if you have faith as
a mustard seed, you will say to this mountain,
"Move from here to there," and it will move;
and nothing will be impossible for you.

MATTHEW 17:20

MY NAME IS George McCormack. I was born in Brooklyn, New York, in 1931. I graduated from Harvard Law School and am a lawyer by trade.

If you read the newspapers nowadays, you know it's viewed as an absolute fact that God never intervenes. Everything is made out to happen by chance, coincidence, science, or something else. In order to provide evidence to refute that line of thinking, I wanted to relate several of the many events that have happened in the life of my wife, Martha, and myself, where our heavenly Father has intervened in some way.

Martha and I were raised Catholic and were very active Catholics. We were involved in the Catholic Charismatic Renewal after the Second Vatican Council. We worked very hard in the Brooklyn Diocese.

When we were about forty years old, we asked God for, and received, the baptism of the Holy Spirit. This was the significant turning point in our lives, because when that happened we began to see things in a different light. Things that we formerly thought were good, we saw were not so good; things we were taught and brought up to think of as being bad, we saw were good in God's sight.

As we were open to the Holy Spirit, we began experiencing the miraculous signs of the Holy Spirit and receiving the effects of some of them ourselves. We experienced healings and deliverances, and we saw God work in mighty ways over the course of our lives.

Some years ago Martha and I were praying together daily saying, "Lord, what do You want us to do with the rest of our lives?" We were approaching seventy years old, and our five sons had all grown, married, and left home.

We occasionally attended a small Pentecostal church, and we knew the pastor, Jesus Lopez, very well. He was filled with the Holy Spirit.

When we visited one day, Pastor Lopez prayed with Martha, knowing nothing about what Martha and I had been praying about together. After praying, he said he'd seen a vision about her. The vision was a picture in his mind of Martha standing in a mud brick building with a thatched roof. It was filled with little black children, and she was teaching and preaching to them.

"Does this mean anything to you?" he asked.

"No," Martha said. It didn't mean anything to me either.

About a month later we received a letter from an old friend. He'd been our trainer in Christian counseling many years before. He and his wife had retired as pastors of their church and had gone to Africa to live in Mukono, Uganda. He asked if we would come and help them with their ministry, as they were getting old, sick, and decrepit.

We both immediately said, "Yes!" It was easy, because the Lord had prepared our hearts in advance. We saw this as the fulfillment of this vision.

We went over there that summer. For more than six summers we've been going there and laying roots. We've had a very successful and, in some cases, miraculous ministry there. The people are so sweet and wonderful. So, less than a year after Pastor Lopez told us about his vision, Martha was indeed teaching African children in a mud schoolhouse building with a thatched roof, just as she appeared in the vision. This was another case of God intervening in our lives.

Our ministry in Uganda was expanded to Sudan, emphasizing the then semiautonomous southern region of the country, what is now the Republic of South Sudan. The people there are suffering terribly as a result of twenty-plus years of warfare with the Muslim north, with about two million people killed. In Uganda they at least have food. In Sudan they have nothing.

Our first time in Sudan we visited a displaced persons camp. The conditions were wretched. There was a camp of about two hundred people lying around in the grass. They had practically no clothing, and there were many women with children.

They'd had nothing to eat for several weeks because of road conditions and other problems that prevented the relief trucks from getting through. The children were covered with flies and suffering with fevers. The mothers couldn't nurse them because they had no nutrition to give them. They were reduced to picking leaves off bushes and trees, boiling them and eating them. This didn't help much, and when we arrived, there weren't many leaves left. They had to keep walking farther and farther to find a tree or bush with leaves.

Martha and I preached to the people through an interpreter. Martha was talking to one woman who was there with her baby. They looked in each other's eyes, and Martha embraced her. It was terrible because they were filthy and had little clothing, but when Martha hugged her, this woman could see the love of Christ in her eyes. She spontaneously gave Martha the only possession she had, which was her sprig of leaves.

In speaking with the people later on with an interpreter, Martha related this story to them, and spoke about how Christ gave everything He had as well. This became the theme of her talk.

There was a priest there who heard Martha speaking and witnessed the incident. He had a satellite phone and called two Christian organizations, one in America and one in Canada, and related the incident to them.

By the time we were preparing to go home from Uganda four days later, the local church there had received from those two Christian organizations a total of $170,000 in donations (which is an enormous sum over there). This would enable the church to bring food to this camp (and many others) in small vehicles. The big vehicles of the Red Cross and United Nations weren't able to get in there. There were several understandable reasons for that, but that's what happened. This was another case of God intervening. Out of one sprig of leaves you can see what God can do if there is love and faith in the equation.

God, our loving Father, is constantly intervening in our lives. I look forward to seeing even more of His miraculous interventions to come!

George McCormack (shown with his wife, Martha, ministering in Uganda) is retired from practicing law but remains active in missions and ministry. He lives with his sons in Brooklyn, New York. His beloved wife, Martha, went to be with Jesus in 2009. For more information, write martha_george@earthlink.net.

47

God's Wildflower

Therefore, if anyone is in Christ, he is a
new creation; old things have passed away;
behold, all things have become new.

2 CORINTHIANS 5:17

MY NAME IS Julie Woodley. I was born in Montana in 1957 and raised in a quiet logging town. I endured much trauma and abuse, and if not for God's amazing love and intervention, I wouldn't have survived.

My father was a wealthy, respectable businessman and an active church member. Unfortunately he also carried a deep rage in his soul, which lay hidden until he came home at night. Behind the walls of our peaceful log home daddy's fury would rain down. I spent much of my childhood terrified.

The abuse started before kindergarten—a constant barrage of shame-filled messages: "You're stupid, no good, and ugly. You'll never amount to anything." I believed my father's words and felt worthless. The feelings of worthlessness intensified later with physical and sexual abuse.

My father began sexually abusing me when I was about six. He told me all fathers and daughters did this. I was so confused because it was the only time he ever showed me affection, hugged me, or said he loved me. He warned me I must never share this "secret" with anybody, and if I did, he would kill me—and he was serious.

Later another relative began sexually abusing me. I thought my identity was to be used by men. So as a child and a teenager I was frequently taken advantage of—by the neighbor boys, by the neighbor man, by my boss.

I couldn't talk to anyone about this. I hoped my mother might help, but she was just as hurtful, with frequent comments such as, "You're stupid," and, "You're so ugly." I felt I was no good and was alive only to satisfy men's sexual desires.

The "secret" and my father's anger held me in a grip of terror. Since I couldn't escape the pain, I learned to numb it. Alcohol and marijuana helped me forget the painful memories, cutting words, constant fear, and my father's rough hands.

There was something even more "magical" than alcohol or marijuana—sex. I used sex to medicate the pain, heal my loneliness, and escape my turmoil-filled home. I wasn't really looking for sex; my little girl's heart just yearned for a father's safe embrace. I longed for something pure and true. Instead, my father communicated a twisted, confusing lesson: love equals sex. So with an addictive hunger I gave myself to men, trying to find real love.

Not surprisingly I became pregnant at seventeen. My parents, horrified of what the neighbors might think, scheduled an appointment at a women's clinic. We drove in silence to Spokane, Washington, to terminate the pregnancy. Abortions still seemed scary and deviant in 1975, but they were legal. The procedure was painful and bloody. I just wanted someone to comfort me. After the abortion we rode home in an empty quietness for five long hours.

My parents' mission was accomplished. I knew I'd committed the unpardonable sin.

My father was livid that I'd become pregnant. He took it out on me in every way. The next eighteen months were filled with violence. On one occasion he barged into my room with a shotgun, threatening to shoot me. I knew I had only two choices: leave or die.

Late that night I climbed out my bedroom window and ran down the mountain wearing only pajamas. I made it to my friend's house, and her father protected me during those last months of high school.

The day after graduation, I walked to the train station at 4:00 a.m. and boarded a train with a one-way ticket, one change of clothes, and no money. I rode the train, crying all the way to Wisconsin.

I thought I could escape my past with new surroundings, but the pain, emptiness, and my addictions followed me. In Wisconsin I met Cathy, my best friend during those bewildering days. With reckless abandon Cathy and I partied, drank, and slept with new guys every weekend. Thinking I could outdistance my past, I kept running. I moved twenty-five times in five years. But my childhood pain and the hurt in my soul kept pace. I drank, took drugs, and slept with many men. This led to another pregnancy and to a second devastating abortion. On top of that Cathy was murdered while hitchhiking in Minnesota.

To cover the grief and pain I made a vow: I would have a different bottle of booze and a different man every night. I kept that vow very well. But one night I didn't have a bottle or a man. I hit rock bottom.

I lay on my bed sobbing, unable to stop. The pain erupted like a volcano. I had a bottle of pills in the medicine cabinet for this "special" night when I would kill myself. I took the pills out and paced around the room like a caged animal. Four times I put the pills back in, only to pull them out again.

I dug my fingernails into my wrist, the skin raw and bloody, to divert my mind from the feelings of pain and hopelessness. I grabbed the pills and threw them in the garbage to stop from committing suicide. After two exhausting hours, I finally cried myself to sleep.

During my sleep, alone in my one-room apartment, I heard a voice. Gradually growing louder and louder the voice kept repeating, "Julie, I love you; Julie, I love you." It was strong and authoritative, yet calm, gentle, and safe. A comforting warmth rushed over me. I should've been afraid, hearing voices in the night, but more than anything I felt loved and cherished.

I had no idea who spoke to me or where the voice came from. I certainly didn't associate it with Jesus Christ. And the words, "Julie, I love you" didn't immediately alter my circumstances. But for two years, every time I felt hopeless that voice returned, gently repeating, "Julie, I love you." I decided to make something of my life, and I enrolled in college.

It was during college several years later that I was invited to a Bible study by some caring Christians. Through their love, guidance, and witness, I found the true love I was searching for in Christ. I learned it was

His voice that had comforted and sustained me during those dark nights of despair.

It's been a long journey of healing, but today I'm secure in my identity as a forgiven and beloved daughter of my heavenly Father. Today I counsel abuse and trauma victims, and God has given me a heart for broken, hurting people. Jesus has done an amazing miracle of restoration in my life. If you're struggling with depression or despair, I encourage you to cry out to Jesus and find a good Christian counselor who can walk with you through the process of forgiveness, healing, and restoration. I'm proof that your life *can* change.

 **Julie Woodley** is the founder and director of Restoring the Heart Ministries Inc. She is a speaker, author, and counselor, and serves as a division chairperson with the American Association of Christian Counselors. Julie has an MA in counseling from Bethel Seminary and is a certified trauma counselor. She travels extensively out of her home base in Florida. For more information, write info@rthm.cc or visit www.rthm.cc.

48

Dead of a Heart Attack, Alive in Christ

I am the resurrection and the
life. He who believes in Me, though
he may die, he shall live.

JOHN 11:25

*M*Y NAME IS Jeff Markin. I was born in 1953 and grew up on Long Island, New York. In 1985 my family moved to Florida, where I still live and work as a mechanic.

I grew up attending a Lutheran church, but many of the people I knew were hypocrites. They'd go to church on Sundays but were abusive to their families or friends. As a result, I shied away from being a weekly worshipper and just believed in God in my own way. I was away from church for many years until something very dramatic happened that changed everything.

On September 20, 2006, I woke up, got ready for work as usual, started the car, and drove off. The last thing I remember was leaving my driveway. The next time I was aware of anything was four days later when I awoke in my daughter's arms in the hospital. I have no waking memory of the events that transpired during the interim, but I later learned what happened.

Apparently I called my boss from the car and told him I wasn't feeling well. He sensed something wasn't right and advised me to drive to Palm Beach Gardens Hospital Medical Center. I parked the car and walked in. As I reached the check-in desk, I collapsed on the floor from a massive heart attack. The ER team rushed out and tried to revive me. It was a miracle that while driving I didn't crash, hurt someone, or even pull over. If that had happened, I wouldn't be here today.

The ER team paged Dr. Chauncey Crandall, the head cardiologist, who was doing rounds that morning. I later learned that he was busy and tired and didn't get down there for about thirty minutes. They weren't having any luck reviving me, and when Dr. Crandall arrived, he found the scene very chaotic. I was turning black from lack of oxygen. He reviewed the paperwork and confirmed they had done all the proper protocols in trying to revive me. He pronounced me dead at around 8:20 a.m.

During this time, I remember being out of my body and standing in the back of a funeral home. The room was empty and I realized I had died. I saw a vision of my own funeral, and thought, "Where is everyone? I thought I was loved, but nobody's here."

The funeral scene then dissipated, and I was staring at extremely bright, white lights that were swirling over me. Suddenly the lights stopped and a figure emerged. It had no hair, and it had large eyes and a pale complexion. I didn't feel threatened. I thought maybe it was my guardian angel there to watch over me.

We communicated nonverbally, and he assured me that everything would be taken care of, that I would be all right, and that he had to go but would return. He went back into the lights and they began to swirl around again. After a while the lights stopped, and he reappeared and told me not to worry, and that I would have a nice life. Then he said he had to go again and went back up into the lights.

Then I experienced a choking, gagging feeling. This was when they were removing the respirator tube from my throat. The next thing I knew, I awoke in my daughter's arms. She told me I was in the hospital and that I'd had a massive heart attack.

My hands and ankles were still dark from cyanosis—they looked badly bruised. I spent ten days in the ICU being stabilized with stents and drugs. Several days after being released from the ICU, I underwent quadruple bypass heart surgery.

After I was settled in the hospital's cardiac wing, Dr. Crandall visited me. He asked if I would pray with him to ask Jesus Christ into my life. I was surprised that a doctor would ask me this, but I said of course I would. We prayed together, then he began telling me what happened—about how bad the heart attack was and that my body had started turning black. The ER team had worked on me for at least thirty minutes, he said, performing CPR and shocking me seven times with no success.

After Dr. Crandall had pronounced me dead and filled out the paperwork, he left to resume his rounds and see other patients. He was suddenly stopped in his tracks by the voice of the Lord. He was told to turn around, go back, and pray for me. He didn't want to, for fear of looking foolish, but God told him again. This time he obeyed. He turned around, went back, and stood by my body.

There was a nurse on the other side of my body looking at him curiously. Dr. Crandall prayed over my dead body, saying, "Father God, I cry out for this man's soul. If he does not know You as Lord and Savior, raise him from the dead now, in Jesus's name." At that moment another doctor walked in, and Dr. Crandall told him, "You need to shock this man again."

He refused initially, but Dr. Crandall persuaded him, saying, "Let's do this once more." You have to understand, by then all the IVs were disconnected, and all the breathing tubes were already out of my body. I'd been declared dead and was black with cyanosis. Nevertheless the ER physician shocked me for the eighth time. Instantly a perfect heartbeat came back!

Dr. Crandall, the other doctor, and the nurse were stunned as they looked at a perfect heartbeat on the monitor. The nurse actually screamed when I started moving. They thought I'd be brain dead or a vegetable, but they rushed me to ICU. They never thought I would survive, but a month later I walked out of the hospital. I'm fully recovered today. The Lord did a miracle. I haven't had any organ or neurological problems. Four months after being discharged, I returned to work full time.

God shined on me with His great love, and I'm so blessed. This incident taught me much about the power of prayer. God's power, prayer, and medical technology all came together miraculously that day. Today I attend church and Bible studies regularly. I got re-baptized and dedicated my life to Jesus. I appreciate every moment I have.

It's a shame that it took the tragedy of a heart attack to bring me to this place in my life, but I almost wish everybody could experience it and survive. Then everyone would really have a special appreciation for life. I'm walking with Jesus, growing, and sharing my testimony with everybody.

Jeff Markin still lives and works as a mechanic in Florida and continues to share his miraculous testimony of Jesus's resurrection power with anyone who will listen. For more information, write jeffmarkin@yahoo.com.

49

From Bombs and Bullets to Bibles and Blessings

Love never fails.

1 Corinthians 13:8

*M*y name is Jacob DeShazer. I'm one of the original Doolittle Raiders who bombed mainland Japan during the Second World War, under Maj. Gen. James Doolittle. After that raid, my crew and I were captured, and I spent forty months as a prisoner of war. I endured torture, starvation, and abuse; but through it all God was with me, and Jesus changed my life.

I was born in Oregon in 1912 to Christian parents. I attended elementary school and high school in Madras, Oregon. I initially learned about God through attending Sunday school and church there.

After graduating high school in 1931, I worked various jobs for several years. Then the Second World War started, and I enlisted in the army in 1939. For two years I trained as an airplane mechanic and bombardier. During that time, army life included much routine and little excitement.

When the Japanese bombed Pearl Harbor on December 7, 1941, everything changed. I heard about the attack on the radio while on KP (kitchen patrol) duty, peeling potatoes at my base in Oregon. I hurled a potato against the wall and screamed, "The Japs will pay for this!" Overnight, hatred for Japan engulfed America. We had entered the war.

After Pearl Harbor our military was driven back with defeats at Wake Island, Guam, the Philippines, and the Java straits. As a way to jar the Japanese leadership, our leaders decided to make an unprecedented raid on the Japanese mainland. I didn't learn of the mission until I volunteered for it. Even then it was classified—the details weren't divulged.

The volunteers began intensive training in aerial maneuvers, low flying, and bombing.

James Doolittle (then a lieutenant colonel) led the mission. On April 2, 1942, the aircraft carrier USS Hornet left San Francisco Bay carrying us and our sixteen B-25 bombers. We joined a convoy of ships headed for Japan.

We encountered three Japanese ships on April 18. To retain the element of surprise, we were ordered to take off prematurely—we were still eight hundred miles from Japan. We knew that with the added distance between us and Japan, there was little chance we would survive the mission.

Our plane made it to Japan, and we successfully bombed some oil tanks and a building that looked like a factory, then headed across the sea to China. It was dark and foggy, we were low on fuel, and finally we were forced to parachute from the plane.

I was separated from my crew and eventually captured by the Japanese. I was reunited with four comrades who also were captured. We later learned that most of the Doolittle Raiders made it to friendly Chinese locations. My crew and three others were captured. And so began forty months of imprisonment and suffering.

We were interrogated constantly, starved, beaten, and tortured. One torture was the "water cure"—water was poured on a wet towel that was placed over a man's open mouth, so when the man gasped for breath he felt like he was drowning. In another method, a long, two-inch-diameter bamboo stick was placed behind the prisoner's knees. He was forced to kneel with folded legs, then a soldier repeatedly jumped on his thighs. My heart burned with intense hatred for the Japanese.

Bedbugs, lice, and rats were plentiful. We were filthy, sick, and emaciated. Three of my comrades were executed, and one died of dysentery. I was discouraged and hopeless. Our requests for more food and news from home were continually denied, but the Japanese eventually did give us some books, including a Bible. I had long since lost interest in the Bible—if, in truth, I'd ever had any interest. Now I greatly desired to read it. I read the entire book through multiple times, spending many hours memorizing it. The Holy Spirit began illuminating God's Word, and Christ was speaking to me.

On June 8, 1944, I read Romans 10:9, "If you confess with your mouth the Lord Jesus and believe in your heart that God has raised Him from the dead, you will be saved." I'd read that passage before, but on that day it somehow became powerful.

I prayed, "Lord, though I'm far from home and imprisoned, I must have forgiveness." As I prayed, I felt a rest in my soul and an inner witness that God had forgiven me. I was joyful! I wouldn't have traded places with anyone right then. What a joy it was to know I was saved, that God had forgiven my sins, and that I'd partaken of the divine nature! (See 2 Peter 1:4.) Starvation, a freezing cell, and even death no longer scared me.

I'd grown weak due to malnutrition and dysentery, lice and bedbugs. I counted more than seventy-five boils on my body. I was miserable. After reading the Bible and becoming a Christian, I thought about how much easier it would be to die and go to heaven than to live and continue suffering.

I raised my hands and said, "Lord, take me. I want to leave this suffering and be with You." Then I noticed my hands were empty, and I thought, "I can't go like this. I've never done anything for the Lord." I put my hands down and said, "Lord, I don't want to come to You empty-handed. Please give me another chance."

I prayed for God's strength and wisdom. I'd read much in the Bible about loving others. I still had the same cruel guards, solitary confinement, and bad food, but my attitude began changing. My comrades noticed, as did the guards. God began melting my heart and removing my hatred of the Japanese. It changed to compassion and a burden to share Christ's love with them. One day as I prayed in my dark cell, the Holy Spirit clearly said, "You are called to teach the Japanese people and to go wherever I send you." I told God I would obey.

Finally, on August 20, 1945, the forty months of imprisonment ended! A Japanese official announced: "The war is over. You can go home." We were very weak but elated.

I returned to America, enrolled in Bible college, and married my wife,

Florence, in 1946. I graduated with a degree in missions two years later. I returned to Japan in December 1948—not as a bombardier, but as a missionary. I now had love and goodwill toward Japan. How much better it is to conquer evil with the gospel of peace!

Florence and I spent thirty years in Japan spreading Christ's message of salvation, love, and forgiveness. We helped start more than twenty churches and saw God move mightily in many people's lives.

God uses many things to bring us around and get us to Him. It's strange that war can be one of those things.

After many years in missions and ministry **Jacob DeShazer** (1912–2008) is now with Jesus. For more information about the life of this incredible man, or to order copies of the most recent book written about him, *Return of the Raider*, contact his daughter Carol Aiko DeShazer Dixon at carolaiko@aol.com or visit www.jacobdeshazer.com.

50

The Christmas Miracle

There was a woman who had a spirit of
infirmity eighteen years, and was bent
over and could in no way raise herself
up. But when Jesus saw her...He laid
His hands on her, and immediately she
was made straight, and glorified God.

LUKE 13:11–13

MY NAME IS Ema McKinley. I was born in Iowa in 1946 and
grew up in a Christian family. I now live in Rochester, Minnesota, and
have two sons and two grandchildren. The Lord has given me a love for
children and the disabled, with whom I have worked for years. In 1993 I
suffered an accident that left me severely disabled. I faced a tremendous
struggle after the accident, but God taught me much through it, and ultimately did an amazing miracle.

I was in the department store where I worked. It was the Saturday
before Easter, in April 1993, and we were preparing the store for the next
week. While getting some things I needed to stock my shelves, I climbed
into a thirty-three-foot-high loft in the storage room. A heater vent
kicked in, the heat overtook me, and I fainted. I fell, but my left leg was
caught between some boards and boxes. My body swung down, causing
me to hit my head on something. I hung upside down and unconscious
for several hours before a coworker found me. The next thing I remember
was waking up in the hospital.

I was confused—I had a concussion and had lost 60 percent of my
hearing. I had tremendous pain in the foot that had been caught and
twisted. After a month my leg healed, but that's when another health

challenge—RSD (reflex sympathetic dystrophy)—started. RSD is a terrible, painful condition that's largely a mystery to the medical community. It affects your muscles and nerves, creating a constant burning sensation, as if you're plugged into a light socket. Pain shoots through your joints, and your skin changes color and temperature.

Medically speaking, there's no cure for RSD. Treatments include nerve blocks and morphine pumps. The doctors ask you to describe your pain level based on a one-to-ten scale, one being minimal pain and ten being maximum. With RSD the pain is off the charts—it's about fifteen! Consequently the suicide rate among RSD patients is high. I have been on twenty-two kinds of medications and up to 2,000 mg of morphine per day, just for pain management. The pain would travel from my hands and feet into my neck and spine. The best doctors in the world did everything they knew to do for me for nineteen years.

My upper torso was twisted, and for fifteen years I literally hung over the side of my wheelchair, unable to straighten up. Doorways needed to be forty inches wide so I could get my head and wheelchair through them. In my home I have custom-built, forty-inch doorways. I was on crutches for three years after the accident, then for the next fifteen years I was in the wheelchair 24/7, hanging over the left side. I didn't sleep in a bed for more than fifteen years.

The large doses of medication prevented me from eating food because I would always bring it up. I didn't eat a meal for more than seventeen years. I lived on nutrient drinks and liquids. I could not sleep because of the pain. I would be awake for about seventy hours straight, until my body would simply shut down for about three hours at a time. Then it would be another seventy hours until I slept again. That's how I lived from 1993 to 2011.

I had loved Jesus since childhood, but after the accident I needed Him even more. I partnered with God—I took one day at a time and renewed my trust in Him daily. I never became angry or depressed because God was with me. I attended church when I could, but persisted in praise and prayer even when I couldn't attend services.

On Christmas Eve 2011 at about 1:00 a.m., something dramatic happened to me. I was sitting at my computer in my office. I turned my wheelchair, and the right wheel came off the floor. The wheelchair tipped and I fell out, landing on my left side. The pain in my spine and neck was excruciating. I was alone in the house, and I lay on the floor in agony, unable to move, for more than *eight hours!* I constantly called out to Jesus, but I was also thinking, "This is how God is going to take me home." I thought He would come and either take me right there or help me in some other way.

Jesus did come after eight-and-a-half hours—and He came miraculously. I didn't see His face, but I saw the most awesome white robe. Human eyes could barely endure looking at it—the light from it was so bright.

I felt Jesus enter my body. For all those years my left foot had been inverted and crooked. A steel bar under my wheelchair held my foot. I felt Jesus straightening that foot. He then went to my left hand, which was completely clenched. I had not opened it for more than sixteen years. The RSD had turned it into a clubhand. Jesus began opening my fingers. When my fingers were fully extended, I saw the inside of my hand was raw flesh. I watched new skin grow over my palm and fingers.

Jesus then worked on my neck and spine. I was able to turn onto my back—and realized my spine was completely straight! The Lord then knelt beside me and offered me His hand. I put my hand in His, and we stood up together. I was standing on feet and legs that I hadn't fully used in eighteen years!

I walked out of my office like a drunken sailor, bumping into furniture and walls, since those muscles hadn't been used in years. I walked to my kitchen and around my house. God had straightened my foot, hand, neck, and spine, and I was walking!

Soon my two sons and grandsons would be coming to my house for Christmas Eve morning. When my family arrived and opened the door, they saw my empty wheelchair first. Seconds later, I walked down the hall. When they saw me walking, they were stunned. My grandson had only known "crooked" Grandma in the wheelchair. My son Jason exclaimed, *"Are you kidding?"* My son Jeffrey turned white. His mouth hung open, and he couldn't speak. I walked up to him and embraced him.

God gave me a miracle. I have my mobility back and I give Jesus all

the glory for my Christmas miracle. I have been given a second chance at life, and I still have much work to do for Him.

My story is being told around the world, and many people have been encouraged by it. I've shared my testimony with many doctors who had become very familiar with me during those nineteen years. When they saw me walking, they were thrilled—and shocked—and some have admitted that what happened to me was a miracle. God is good!

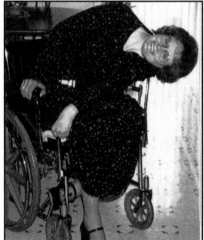

| Ema in her wheelchair, post accident, mid-1990s | Ema, in 2012, standing tall after her healing |

Ema McKinley today continues her life of ministry from her home in Rochester, Minnesota. Since her healing, she has been traveling and sharing her testimony at conferences, churches, and events nationwide. The full account of her unforgettable story is available in her 2014 book, *A Rush of Heaven* (www.Zondervan.com). For more information, write soaringspirit24@yahoo.com. To view medical documentation, see Appendix.

Conclusion

*W*HILE IT IS interesting to read about other people's divine interventions and experiences with God, it is much more important to know that you, personally, are going to heaven. If you have never trusted Christ as your Savior, or if you are not sure that you are going to heaven, let me share with you very simply what the Bible says about how to go to heaven.

I was raised in the Lutheran Church and have believed in God since I was a child. I knew about heaven and hell, but I didn't know if I was going to heaven; I didn't fully understand what Christ did for me on the cross. I remember as a teenager that the thought of death and hell sometimes frightened me so much it would keep me awake at night. When I was fifteen years old, my brother asked me, "Daniel, if you were to die today, do you know for sure that you would go to heaven?"

I said, "No, I don't." I had been baptized, catechized, "pasteurized," and "homogenized"! Yet I still feared death and hell. I really wasn't sure of my eternal destination. My brother shared some scriptures with me from the Bible, and I finally understood what God wanted. Much of what I had learned in my Lutheran upbringing came together for me then.

The Bible says in Romans 3:23, "For all have sinned and fall short of the glory of God." My brother explained to me that as a sinner, I had done things God didn't like. I had to agree with him there.

"The Bible says that everyone is a sinner," he explained. "Some people are worse than others in man's eyes, but in God's eyes one sin makes you a sinner. You're in trouble if you've broken only one of God's laws."

He also showed me Romans 6:23, "The wages of sin is death," and explained: "Wages is something you earn, so this means that what you have earned because of your sin is the death penalty. You deserve to die and go to hell. The problem is that God loves you, and He doesn't want you to go to hell. In order to be just, God has to punish sin, but because

He loves us, He decided to provide a way out. Jesus Christ came down from heaven to die on the cross to pay for your sins, and now you can accept what He did for you. So actually His death paid for your sin."

Romans 6:23 goes on to say, "But the gift of God is eternal life through Jesus Christ our Lord." You do not get eternal life through the church; you don't get it from being baptized or by being good. You get eternal life through Jesus Christ. We received from our parents the free gift of physical life. Somebody else did the work, went through the pain, paid all the bills, and you and I got a free gift—physical life. It takes only a few minutes to be born. Growing takes a long time.

Similarly, being born into God's family takes only a few minutes, but growing in God's family takes a long time and requires a lot of effort, such as reading your Bible, going to church, and praying. Those things help you grow as a Christian, but they don't make you a Christian. You become a Christian only if one person does the work for you—Jesus Christ. He comes and lives in your heart and makes you a new person.

My brother explained all that to me—I deserved eternal death because of my sin, but God loved me, and He wanted to give me eternal life.

"How do I get it?" I asked. He then showed me Romans 10:13: "For 'whoever calls on the name of the LORD shall be saved.'" It doesn't say you might be saved—it says you *shall* be saved. Anybody who receives Jesus Christ—they call on Him; they ask Him into their lives—will be saved.

John 1:12 says that if you receive Him, you become a child of God. John 3:3 says that you *must* be born again. These things all tie together. When you receive Christ as your Savior—some people use the expression, "You receive Him into your heart"—and accept what He has done for you in dying for your sins, you become a child of God. You receive a new birth. It just takes a few moments to say, "Jesus, I am a sinner. Would You please forgive me and save me?"

That day back in 1990 I bowed my head and said, "Lord, I'm a sinner. I believe You died for me on the cross, and I believe You rose from the dead. I'd like You to forgive me. I'd like You to come live in my heart and save me. Please make me a new person." I received Christ as my Savior. That day became my spiritual birthday into the family of God.

I am now a child of God, and if I do something wrong, I cannot go to hell because I have received the gift of eternal life, and eternal life lasts forever. But as God's child, I can still receive God's discipline and correction. You see, I am in the family now, and if I commit some sin, it's treated very differently than it would have been before. It's a family matter now; whereas, if I sinned before, God would have been my judge. It would have been a legal matter. Now when I tell people I am going to heaven, I know it is not because I am so good, but because my sins have been paid for.

You can have the same thing. If you'll accept Jesus Christ as your Savior right now, He'll forgive your sin, save you, and take you to heaven when your journey here is over. So please, check your heart. Tomorrow is promised to no one. If you have not trusted Christ as your Savior, why don't you ask Him to save you right now? Just bow your head and pray a simple prayer like I prayed in 1990. There are no magic words—God knows what is in your heart. If you would like to receive Christ, pray a prayer like the following:

Dear Lord Jesus, I know that I am a sinner. I believe You died for me on the cross. I believe You rose from the dead, and I would like to ask You to forgive me and save me. I now receive You as my Savior, in Jesus's name. Amen.

Remember, Romans 10:13 says, "For 'whoever calls on the name of the LORD shall be saved.'" If you've just received Christ, you have God's promise that you are going to heaven, and God's promises last forever.

When you receive Jesus as your Savior, you are born into God's family. That's just the beginning—growing will require a lot of work. You're going to need to read your Bible, pray, start telling other people about Jesus, and more. Doing those things will help you to grow and become a strong disciple of Christ.

If you've just accepted Christ as your Savior, please write me and let me know so I can rejoice with you. I'll be glad to help if I can.

I hope you have enjoyed this book. God bless you!

Appendix

Chapter 8
Shot Forty-Three Times
Derrick Holmes

```
CEDARS-SINAI MEDICAL CENTER, LOS ANGELES, CA

              PATIENT: HOLMES, DERRICK
              MED REC: ██████████
              DICTATOR: JORDAN H. GOODSTEIN, M.D.


CONSULTATION - GENERAL SURGERY
01/20/98
****************** ATTENTION:  DISCLAIMER NOTE ******************




************************************************************************

CC:

CONSULTANT: JORDAN H. GOODSTEIN, M.D.

The patient was admitted on 01/18/98 through the emergency room.  He
was the victim of a gunshot assault, with multiple shotgun and gunshot
wounds.  He was noted to have hypotension in the ER with massive
injuries to both lower extremities, including significant fractures in
the below knee area on the left, in the femur on the right, and in the
hip on the right.  In addition, there were multiple pellets in the
retroperitoneum on the left.  There was some significant gluteal
injury on the right side.  Both upper extremities had soft tissue
injuries secondary to gunshot wounds, with open wounds, but no
fractures.  There was a scrotal injury with penetrating wound at the
base of the penis, as well.  The patient was intubated and
resuscitated in the emergency room.  I was contacted and came to the
hospital to take the patient to surgery for a laparotomy.  It was
reported that he had a diffusely tender abdomen, and x-ray of the
abdomen showed multiple pellets in the retroperitoneum and possibly
within the peritoneal cavity.  He was given repeated blood
transfusions during resuscitation and required six units of blood in
preparation for his laparotomy.  At the laparotomy, he was found to
have a retroperitoneal hematoma with significant bleeding in the area
of the iliac vessel and iliopsoas.  The hematoma was open, and the
left kidney and ureter were explored and found to be free of injury.
The patient had had some hematuria prior to surgery.  The hematoma was
drained and the iliac vein was determined to be uninjured.  Finally,
the abdomen was closed and the orthopedic and vascular surgeons
evaluated the patient and treated his orthopedic injuries.  The
patient was transferred to the intensive care unit for postoperative
management.



DICTATOR: JORDAN H. GOODSTEIN, M.D.
```

Chapter 18
An Islamic Warrior Finds Peace in Christ
Zachariah Anani

MEDICAL REPORT FOR ZAKARIA H ANNANI

THIS 33 YEAR OLD LEBANESE MAN HAS SUFFERED MULTIPLE INJURIES FROM RELIGIOUS AND POLITICAL PERSECUTION IN LEBANON. BELOW ARE THE FINDINGS OF AN EXAMINATION PERFORMED IN MY OFFICE ON 10/25/96.

HISTORY:

THIS MAN'S INJURIES DATE FROM 1974 AND WERE LISTED AS FOLLOWS:

1974 - KNIFE WOUND UPPER LIP, UNDER NOSE
1976 - BOUND AND THROWN ONTO A LARGE POINTED STICK WHICH PENETRATED INTO THE RECTUM
BLUNT INJURY TO LEFT KNEE, REQUIRING SURGICAL REMOVAL OF MENISCUS (CARTILAGE)
1977 - KNIFE WOUND TO LEFT EYEBROW AND BLUNT INJURY TO LEFT TEMPLE
1978 - BLUNT INJURY TO TOP OF HEAD
1979 - GUNSHOT WOUND TO ABDOMEN, REQUIRING ABDOMINAL SURGERY AND REMOVAL OF PORTIONS OF INTESTINES
1983 - KNIFE WOUND TO BACK OF NECK AND LEFT ELBOW
1995 - PENETRATING INJURY TO LEFT ANKLE AND RESULTING FRACTURE

PHYSICAL EXAM:

HEENT - 4 CM SCAR TOP OF SCALP FROM BLUNT INJURY
2.5 CM SCAR LEFT EYEBROW FROM KNIFE INJURY
SCAR LEFT TEMPLE FROM BLUNT INJURY
1 CM SCAR AT MEDIAL RIGHT NARES FROM KNIFE
5.5 CM SCAR ON LEFT NECK - SURGICAL FROM KNIFE INJURY

ABDOMEN - LARGE CENTRAL STELLATE SCAR WITH CENTRAL DEPRESSION AND SURGICAL SCAR ALONGSIDE FROM SHOOTING INJURY

PERIANAL - LARGE AREA SURROUNDING THE ANUS FROM PENETRATING INJURY

EXTREMITIES - 2.5 CM SCAR AT BASE OF PALM FROM KNIFE INJURY
2.5 CM SCAR IN THE ANTECUBITAL FOSSA FROM KNIFE INJURY
SURGICAL SCAR MEDIAL LEFT KNEE FROM MENISCAL REMOVAL

SINCERELY,

DANIEL W. THOMPSON, M.D.
FAMILY MEDICINE

Chapter 22
Stepping Out in Faith
Denise Lotierzo-Block

SOUTH SHORE NEUROLOGIC
ASSOCIATES, P.C.

HENRY MORETA, MD
MARK GUDESBLATT, MD
STEVEN ROSEN, MD
DAVID L. BESSER, MD
SAMSON MEBRAHTU, MD
NORMAN PFLASTER, MD
HUGH XIAN, MD, PhD
EDWARD FIROUZTALE, DO, DSc
MYASSAR ZARIF, MD
MICHAEL Z. GUO, MD, PhD
PHILIPPE VAILLANCOURT, MD
BHUPINDER SINGH ANAND, MD
AGHA RAZA, MD
JOSHUA J. WEAVER, MD

PATIENT: Denise Block
DATE OF BIRTH:
DATE: 05/16/2013 01:15 PM
HISTORIAN: patient
VISIT TYPE: Office Visit
DOCUMENT TYPE: Chart Note

History of Present Illness:
This 54 year old female presents with:
1. TIA vs seizure
The symptoms began on 02/15/2013 and generally lasts 45 to 60 minutes. The symptoms are reported as being severe. The symptoms occur once. The location is head. Aggravating factors include nothing. Relieving factors include self-resolved. She states the symptoms have resolved.

This is a 53 year-old woman who I saw in hospital followup on 3/7/13 for episode of word-finding difficulty.

INITIAL HISTORY: She had sharp onset pain in her head and a transient episode of being unable to say many common words. This lasted a little under an hour. She was hospitalized due to these symptoms coupled with her history of prior subdural hematoma and surgical drainage; the concern was for possible TIA versus seizure and she was worked up for this with scans and EEG as well as telemetry monitoring. Days after she left the hospital, she has had a few episodes of word-finding difficulty which is very unusal for her. It would take her all day to remember very common words and this was frightening for her. She was previously seen in our office on 4/25/2007 for progressively worsening b/l neck pain, L > R shoulder pain. She has a history of traumatic right SDH requiring surgical drainage. She also had trauma to neck and shoulders as well. She had PT in the past and this helped. History of left shoulder bursitis and associated tendonitis and rotator cuff syndrome.

Surgery for the subdural hematoma in 2002; immediately after the surgery she had mild forgetfulness which resolved. She was in perfect health with no memory problems, working as an accountant for many years prior to this event that occurred on 2/14/13. This event was extremely concerning for seizure vs TIA especially given her prior subdural/cerebral injury and neurosurgical procedure.

INTERVAL HISTORY:

She has been doing well since the last visit. No further episodes of word-finding difficulty. Infrequent headaches.

Block, Denise   1/4

Chapter 34
Our God Is a Living God
Mathew John

Neurosurgery - Outpt Record   JOHN, MATHEW - ▮▮▮▮▮

* Final Report *

Result Type: Neurosurgery - Outpt Record
Service Date: July 05, 2006 00:00
Result Status: Authenticated
Result Title: ▮
Performed By: Sekhar, MD, Laligam Natarajan on July 05, 2006 16:50
Verified By: Sekhar, MD, Laligam Natarajan on July 06, 2006 18:42
Encounter info: ▮▮▮▮ HMC, Outpatient, 07/05/2006 - 07/05/2006

* Final Report *

DATE OF BIRTH:
▮▮▮▮

SUBJECTIVE:
This patient had been admitted to the Harborview Medical Center on the Neurology Service last week with meningitis. This was secondary to chronic CSF rhinorrhea that he sustained after the treatment of a pituitary tumor. He was very ill for a while. The meningitis has since then been treated and resolved, and he presents now for definitive treatment of the chronic CSF leakage.

PAST MEDICAL HISTORY:
In 1998 he was operated on by Dr. George Kovoor at Trichur Heart Hospital in India via a left frontal craniotomy to remove a pituitary tumor. Following this the patient had decreased vision in his left eye. After this he completed radiation therapy in multiple sessions. In 1999 he had a sudden improvement of his vision in the left eye, although not back to normal. The patient had decided at the time of serious illness to give up his job and to serve God. He was admitted to the Bible College in the United States and has been working as missionary since that time. In 2002 he started to have sudden bleeding through the nose and it appeared that the tumor had dissolved and come out through the nose. He had an MRI scan performed at that time which found that there was little tumor left. However, about the same time the patient developed chronic CSF rhinorrhea which initially he felt was nasal secretion, but it turned out to be CSF. His first and only episode of meningitis was recently.

ALLERGIES:
None.

MEDICATIONS:
1.   Prednisone 5 mg once a day.
2.   Multivitamin one tablet once a day.
3.   Tylenol 650 mg every 6 hours.
4.   Ibuprofen 600 mg three times a day.

Printed by: Kellison-Bullard, Ilona M
Printed on: 11/09/2007 12:19

Chapter 41
The Miracle of Hannah
Sandra Rivera

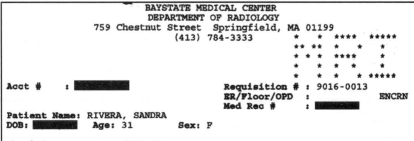

BAYSTATE MEDICAL CENTER
DEPARTMENT OF RADIOLOGY
759 Chestnut Street Springfield, MA 01199
(413) 784-3333

Acct #   :   Requisition # : 9016-0013
                                         ER/Floor/OPD :   ENCRN
                                         Med Rec #   :

Patient Name: RIVERA, SANDRA
DOB: Age: 31   Sex: F

Physician: HAAG, BURRITT MD
Order: BRAIN WITHOUT AND WITH CONTRAST
Signs & Symptoms: lnchk1~Clinical Question:

Physician: HAAG, BURRITT MD   Exam Date: 01/16/97
Primary: UNGAR, JAY   Interpret: 01/17/97
                                    Transcribed: 01/17/97

MRI OF THE PITUITARY WITHOUT AND WITH CONTRAST 1/16/97.

Spin echo T1 sagittal and coronal and fast spin echo proton density and
T2 coronal images of the pituitary and parasellar region were obtained
prior to gadolinium enhancement. Following gadolinium enhancement with
10cc's of intravenous magnevist spin echo T1 coronal images of the
pituitary were performed. Comparison is made with the prior CT scans of
12/93 and 3/94 and 5/95. The mass in the right side of the pituitary
continues to regress and is no longer visualized on the current MRI.
Within the posterior aspect of the pituitary fossa directly adjacent to
the clivus in the midline and slightly to the right of midline there is
a 1.5mm. in AP dimension x 6mm. in diameter of CSF equivalent signal
compatible with concavity of the dorsum related to remodeling by the
previously larger tumor or very tiny slit-like cystic space created by
the regression of the tumor. The gland height is normal. The
diaphragma sella has a gentle downward concavity. The infundibulum is
normal in size and in the midline. The cavernous sinus, suprasellar
cistern, and remainder of the brain appear normal.

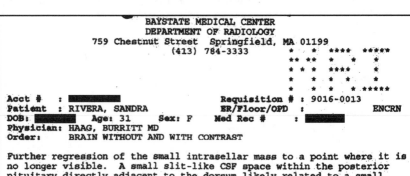

BAYSTATE MEDICAL CENTER
DEPARTMENT OF RADIOLOGY
759 Chestnut Street Springfield, MA 01199
(413) 784-3333

Acct #   :   Requisition # : 9016-0013
Patient   : RIVERA, SANDRA   ER/Floor/OPD :   ENCRN
DOB: Age: 31   Sex: F   Med Rec #   :
Physician: HAAG, BURRITT MD
Order: BRAIN WITHOUT AND WITH CONTRAST

Further regression of the small intrasellar mass to a point where it is
no longer visible. A small slit-like CSF space within the posterior
pituitary directly adjacent to the dorsum likely related to a small
space left by the regression of the tumor.

Chapter 50
The Christmas Miracle
Ema McKinley

 MAYO CLINIC

Patient Copy

Primary Care Internal Medicine

2-695-095 08-Feb-2012 14:25
Ms. Ema Leora McKinley

Limited Evaluation

Generated: 10-Mar-2014 13:46

Page 1 of 4

DEMOGRAPHIC INFORMATION
Clinic Number: 2-695-095
Patient Name: Ms. Ema Leora McKinley
Age: 65 Y
Birthdate: █████████
Address: ████████████████████████

Service Date/Time: 08-Feb-2012 14:25
Provider: David G. Bell, MD Pager: 4-6367
Service: PCIM Type/Desc: LE Status: Fnl Revision #: 2

REFERRAL
Self-referred.

CHIEF COMPLAINT/PURPOSE OF VISIT
Evaluate medical condition.

List of concerns.

HISTORY OF PRESENT ILLNESS
Ms. McKinley comes with her caregiver and her son to discuss medication and related concerns in the context of her long-standing widespread complex regional pain syndrome. Last visit with me was January 4, 2012.

Her medical history is significant for widespread CRPS, RSD-related bullous skin disorder, GERD, odynophagia, and right upper extremity carpal tunnel syndrome.

In the past she has also followed with Dr. Bengtson in PM&R and Hand Clinic; and Dr. Clark Otley, in Dermatology. We have also reviewed her recent PM&R consultation with Dr. Stolp on January 18, 2012. Remotely in Pain Clinic with Dr. Rho, November 12, 2007.

She continues on chronic high-dose narcotics for pain management. Her experimental thalidomide was tapered and discontinued in late 2010.

CURRENTLY
#1 Complex regional pain syndrome
#2 Joint contractures
#3 Deconditioning
In review, she had a work accident about two decades ago, hung upside down from her left foot and ankle for several hours, leading to a global pain problem that involved all extremities, teeth, and jaw. She was followed here in PM&R, and was given the diagnosis of chronic regional pain syndrome for many years. She has been wheelchair-bound for over a decade with an unusual posture, leaning far to the left, only able to use her right upper extremity, even sleeping in this position. She was quite dependent in self cares and still requires high dose narcotics for pain management.

Then she had an extraordinary recovery on Christmas Eve, as we discussed on our last visit. She had accidentally fallen out of her wheelchair and was on the floor alone for several hours before feeling God in her body and straightening out her hand, foot, and spine. She felt that she saw God, and that he knelt beside her, took her hand, and entered her limbs, and that evening she was able to stand up and walk a little bit, although extraordinarily ataxic and incoordinated.

She has maintained that improvement since Christmas. She saw Dr. Stolp in PM&R on January 18, and also had a brief visit with her long-time CRPS physician, Dr. Keith Bengtson, on January 31. ☐

About the Author

$\mathcal{D}$ANIEL FAZZINA, A native New Yorker, is the host of the *Divine Intervention Radio Show*, which can be heard on radio stations across America and at www.divineinterventionradio.com. He attended St. John's University in New York City, where he earned a bachelor's degree in communications in 1998 and served on the university's chapter of InterVarsity Christian Fellowship. As a media-production professional today Daniel has edited music videos, produced award-winning commercials and radio shows, and directed a short film. Daniel's own personal testimony of miraculous healings—from a painful, chronic back condition in 2001 and from a massive, cancerous tumor in 2002—led him to start the *Divine Intervention Radio Show*, for which he interviews intriguing people who have experienced the hand of God in amazing ways. He and his magnificent bride, Sahani, and their lovable Cavalier King Charles spaniel/papillon/Jack Russell terrier, Pumpkin, live in Virginia. Daniel's additional interests include biblical apologetics, creation science, alternative-fuel technologies, auto mechanics, screenwriting, science fiction, classic cars, and cryptozoology.

For more information, contact:

Daniel Fazzina
P.O. Box 70905
Henrico, VA 23255

divineintervention@mail.com
www.divineinterventionradio.com
www.facebook.com/divineinterventionradio
Twitter: @DanielFazzina1

EMPOWERED
TO RADICALLY CHANGE
YOUR WORLD

Charisma House brings you books, e-books, and other media from dynamic Spirit-filled Christians who are passionate about God.

Check out all of our releases from best-selling authors like **Jentezen Franklin**, **Perry Stone**, and **Kimberly Daniels** and experience God's supernatural power at work.

**CHARISMA
HOUSE**

www.charismahouse.com
twitter.com/charismahouse • facebook.com/charismahouse

FREE NEWSLETTERS
TO HELP EMPOWER YOUR LIFE

Why subscribe today?

☐ **DELIVERED DIRECTLY TO YOU.** All you have to do is open your inbox and read.

☐ **EXCLUSIVE CONTENT.** We cover the news overlooked by the mainstream press.

☐ **STAY CURRENT.** Find the latest court rulings, revivals, and cultural trends.

☐ **UPDATE OTHERS.** Easy to forward to friends and family with the click of your mouse.

CHOOSE THE E-NEWSLETTER THAT INTERESTS YOU MOST:

- Christian news
- Daily devotionals
- Spiritual empowerment
- And much, much more

SIGN UP AT: **http://freenewsletters.charismamag.com**

8178

the glory for my Christmas miracle. I have been given a second chance at life, and I still have much work to do for Him.

My story is being told around the world, and many people have been encouraged by it. I've shared my testimony with many doctors who had become very familiar with me during those nineteen years. When they saw me walking, they were thrilled—and shocked—and some have admitted that what happened to me was a miracle. God is good!

| Ema in her wheelchair, post accident, mid-1990s | Ema, in 2012, standing tall after her healing |

Ema McKinley today continues her life of ministry from her home in Rochester, Minnesota. Since her healing, she has been traveling and sharing her testimony at conferences, churches, and events nationwide. The full account of her unforgettable story is available in her 2014 book, *A Rush of Heaven* (www.Zondervan.com). For more information, write soaringspirit24@yahoo.com. To view medical documentation, see Appendix.